Also by Lisa Cherry:

The Brightness of Stars:
Stories from Care Experienced Adults to Inspire Change, 3rd edition,
9781032191584

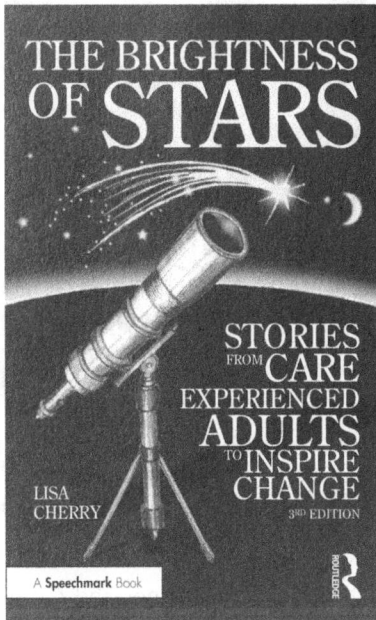

In this poignant book, Lisa Cherry brings together a collection of candid and personal reflections on the care system in the UK, offering alternative ways of thinking about the care experience, supporting better ways of working and providing justification for a trauma-informed lens to be applied to all forms of work with those in care. Whilst each story is unique, shared themes reveal the truth of the care system and, coming at a time where there is a real opportunity for change, the narratives in this book are ultimately stories of hope and connection. This is crucial reading for policy makers, those working in social work, education and adoption, as well as care-experienced adults.

Conversations that Make a Difference for Children and Young People: Relationship-Focused Practice from the Frontline, 9780367644017

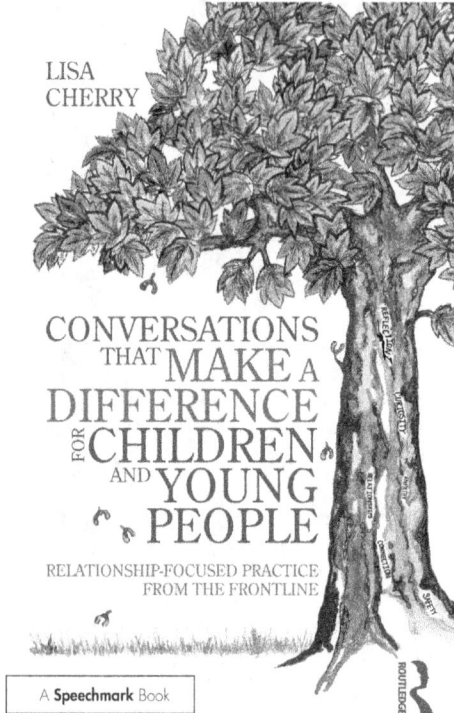

LISA
CHERRY

CONVERSATIONS
THAT MAKE A
DIFFERENCE
FOR CHILDREN
AND YOUNG
PEOPLE

RELATIONSHIP-FOCUSED PRACTICE
FROM THE FRONTLINE

A **Speechmark** Book

In this unique book, international trainer and consultant Lisa Cherry invites professionals from education, social work and healthcare to engage in conversations on a range of pertinent topics and issues affecting children and young people today. By encouraging collaboration between sectors and exploring a range of intersecting themes, the conversations take the reader on a winding journey to broaden their depth of thinking, reflect on their practice and consider the central message: that we can bring about social change, one interaction at a time. This is a must-read for everyone working with children and young people.

Weaving a Web of Belonging

The need to belong is a fundamental and human motivation yet many children and young people's experiences of belonging are ruptured across many domains. This essential book explores the different spaces in which children and young people belong and shows how we can cultivate a sense of belonging within our services, schools and communities and within children themselves.

Chapters break down key research and introduce practices which will inspire change, develop a trauma-informed culture and show how a relational web of belonging can be built for life. Drawing from the lived experiences of those who have spent time in care, the book highlights everything you need to deepen your understanding of the impact of trauma, inequity and marginalisation in children's services and education. Advocating for the power of language, leadership and collective care, a working conceptual model for cultivating belonging is shared, which considers the FACES, SPACES and PLACES that can make a lasting difference. Reflections and practical takeaways are woven throughout to offer an accessible, informative and thoughtful read, with the child at the centre.

Bringing together professional practice, the 'science' behind it and powerful lived experiences, *Weaving a Web of Belonging* offers a true insight into cultivating belonging as an antidote to trauma. It is an essential read for all those who are supporting children and young people, especially those who are the most vulnerable, including education practitioners, leaders, social workers, Children and Adolescent Mental Health Services (CAMHS) and families.

Dr Lisa Cherry is a leading international trainer, specialising in assisting professionals working with vulnerable children and families to understand trauma, recovery and resilience. She is the Director of Trauma Informed Consultancy Services, an organisation which provides a holistic approach to supporting those working in universal, targeted or specialist settings, services and systems. Lisa brings nearly three decades of working in educational and social care settings and a 30-year journey of recovery in overcoming her own experiences of trauma.

"Those of us who have followed Dr Lisa Cherry's work for years look to her for a call to action—and *Weaving a Web of Belonging* is exactly that. But it is also something more: a generous invitation to pause, to reflect, and to rethink how we create spaces of connection. Lisa holds us entangled in a new understanding of belonging that lingers long after the final page."

Tim Fisher, *Principal Social Worker and Relational Activist*

"There is a quiet academic feel about this book, interwoven with lived experiences. This is a real strength and helps set the tone of bringing all that we are, with us. *Weaving a Web of Belonging* focuses not just on our experiences of the past but informs us of the future too."

Sarah Johnson, *Author, Director of Phoenix Education Consultancy and PRUsAP President*

"Lisa is a thought leader. She has a handle on all the research, past and present, and she has lived experience. This is one of the best books I've read on this topic."

Catrina Lowri, *Neurodiversity Trainer and Consultant, Neuroteachers*

"This is an evidence-informed contribution that also recognises the importance of lived experience. There are numerous 'hooks' throughout the book that help to conceptualise belonging and unbelonging with a focus on the care experience. The author writes with passion and provides provocations throughout to make changes that empower and humanise the education, social care and health experience."

Kerry Murphy, *Early Childhood and Inclusion Specialist*

Weaving a Web of Belonging

Developing a Trauma-Informed Culture for All Children

Lisa Cherry

Routledge
Taylor & Francis Group

LONDON AND NEW YORK

Designed cover image: © Dani Pasteau

First published 2025
by Routledge
4 Park Square, Milton Park, Abingdon, Oxon OX14 4RN

and by Routledge
605 Third Avenue, New York, NY 10158

Routledge is an imprint of the Taylor & Francis Group, an informa business

© 2025 Lisa Cherry

The right of Lisa Cherry to be identified as author of this work has been asserted in accordance with sections 77 and 78 of the Copyright, Designs and Patents Act 1988.

All rights reserved. No part of this book may be reprinted or reproduced or utilised in any form or by any electronic, mechanical, or other means, now known or hereafter invented, including photocopying and recording, or in any information storage or retrieval system, without permission in writing from the publishers.

Trademark notice: Product or corporate names may be trademarks or registered trademarks, and are used only for identification and explanation without intent to infringe.

British Library Cataloguing-in-Publication Data
A catalogue record for this book is available from the British Library

ISBN: 978-1-032-73084-4 (hbk)
ISBN: 978-1-032-73081-3 (pbk)
ISBN: 978-1-003-42659-2 (ebk)

DOI: 10.4324/9781003426592

Typeset in Optima
by Deanta Global Publishing Services, Chennai, India

Contents

Contents

Contents

Foreword

It may come as a surprise that Lisa has asked an early career researcher with research expertise in Chinese global citizenship education to write the foreword for her book *Weaving the Web of Belonging*.

However, a closer look at our underlying motives for conducting our research which our supervisor, Professor Alis Oancea, describes as 'source experiences' (2012) are, at the heart, almost one and the same. Indeed, drawing on and articulating these 'source experiences' creates opportunities for interdisciplinarity between scholars, and can bridge the nebulous divide between 'theory' and 'practice'.

Throughout my personal and professional life, I have grappled with the question of belonging and care, in schools, universities, faith settings, homes and as a personal project to make sense of the wounding and wonder a person encounters in life.

With the aid of the 'triad of knowledge', a synthesis of academic, professional and personal knowledges, Lisa has crystallised much of this grappling with and hunger for belonging and care into a comprehensive narrative. These knowledges will provide you with practical wisdom, historical understanding, theoretical insights and personal stories to guide you on your path of 'weaving' the different 'belongings' in the systems, and with the young people and children you work with.

Though Lisa draws extensively from her PhD research, her theoretical conceptualisations of belonging remain grounded in the day-to-day.

Her conceptualisations of 'FACES, SPACES and PLACES' provides a tangible vision for what is needed if young people are to *feel* as if they belong to a family, community, school and local context. She offers a vocabulary and framing to think about the hum-drum encounters of day-to-day life, and that such encounters create the very fabric of meaning and purpose for young people and children.

Setting aside an abstract theorisation of concepts, Lisa instead asks us to reflect and work through how we might enact principles of care and belonging in our vocabulary, behaviour and relational and structural environments, concluding each chapter with Key Chapter Takeaways and evocative questions to help deepen understanding and practice.

Taking a historical perspective to look at both legislation and policy, we are also shown how distorted and harmful framings for those who were raised in care still linger in our current policy imagination and vocabulary. Lisa interrogates such framings, contrasting them with other international contexts, but still acknowledges the UK's key governmental bodies' *attempt* to adopt more inclusive language for the care-experienced community.

Throughout the book, you will notice that Lisa refers to her PhD 'data' as a 'gift' of stories from her participants. These stories are indeed a gift (incidentally, 'data's' root word *datum* means 'to give', pointed out by our other astute supervisor, Dr Nigel Fancourt). It is rare to have in-depth and first-hand accounts from those who grew up in care centred in academic discourse or civil society. However, with Lisa's careful facilitation and understanding of the intersectional experiences those in care go through, her conversation partners reflect back on their life-course to draw out moments of rupture and belonging in institutionalised care settings, schools and wider environments. The participants' searing reflections on experiences such as school exclusion, racism and classism, run in parallel with Lisa's own *source experiences*, and generate a compelling call to engage with the work of care and belonging beyond metrics and policy jargon, further aiding us to become trauma-informed.

I am struck by how this work of 'weaving' implies gentle hands: dexterous, patient and attentive to the tapestry in front of us. In your own learning of how to weave a web of belonging, my hope is that this book will be actively scribbled in, ear-marked and become tattered in its continual use for day-to-day practice in the settings you work in, and be used as a reflective manual to consider *how* and *why* you engage with vulnerable young people and children. Creating the conditions for genuine relational and systemic belonging, particularly for those who have grown up in care, will require a collective Herculean effort, vision and will. However, this is the work our beleaguered societies, worn out with old models, harmful ideologies and vocabularies, demand of us.

May this book spur you on to weave this web of belonging for children and young people with an open heart, clear vision and attentive hands.

Dr Arzhia Habibi, Oxford, 2024

Reference

Oancea, A. (2012). Philosophy of education. In J. Arthur & A. Peterson (Eds.), *The Routledge Companion to Education*. London: Routledge.

Collective Care

What brought you to this book could have been your own experiences of belonging or 'unbelonging', perhaps you've read my other books, have been at my training or heard me deliver a keynote and some of what I say provides resonance. Resonance is a beautiful thing and a lever of connection and safety so if that's the reason, trust that I can feel that from you as you read. Maybe you arrived here because of your journey of learning around the impact of trauma and adversity. This may be from your own traumas or through supporting children and young people living with trauma and adversity, or both. Whatever the reason, you are very welcome here. Coming together as a community so that we can hold the space for one another as we shift the paradigm from problematising and medicalising people, to nurturing and supporting and connecting with people is where the real magic happens ....

As we do this, we must be kind and gentle with ourselves. A tall order in a complex world, working in the public sector which is a whirlwind of busyness and decision making and, at times, carries the burden of moral distress as we can be left making decisions that we feel are not in the best interests of those we are seeking to serve.

Some of the testimonies in this book might feel jarring and upsetting. I urge you to take care. There are many themes described from time to time that would require a 'trigger warning'. Only you know what you can tolerate. If you need a little grounding exercise, I have added one right here that you can return to at any time. Thank you for all you do and all you are yet to do.

GROUNDING EXERCISE

Body Awareness

The purpose of this exercise is to bring you back to the 'now', really important if your mind has been taken to the past or to a place your mind had forgotten but your body had not. By placing the focus on the body, you can be brought back to the here and now.

1. Get in touch with your breath by taking five long, deep breaths through your nose, and exhale through puckered lips.
2. Ensure that both feet are flat on the floor. If the sun is shining, take off your shoes and use the earth under your feet. Feel the sensation by developing awareness of your toes and how your feet feel flat on the ground, ideally in the grass.

3. Allow yourself to lift your feet on and off the ground, almost stomping. Notice how it feels.

4. Now turn to your hands. Clench your hands into fists, then release the tension. Repeat this ten times.

5. Now turn to your hands. Allow your fingertips to touch, gently pressing them together. Allow your touching thumbs to rest in your sternum, that place in the centre of your chest. Press and release, repeating as many times as you choose.

6. Finally, take a tall stretch and reach for the sky. Stretch like this for as long as you choose and slowly release.

Take five more deep breaths and notice the feeling of calm in your body.

Acknowledgements

So much of who I am and what I bring can be attributed to my beautiful adult cubs, Zak and Saskia; the people I belong to.

None of this book would have been possible without the gifts of wisdom given by the participants in my doctorate.

As I entered into the last phases of this book, I underwent a stem cell transplant and Jessica Parker gifted her time to support, proofread and edit where I could be misunderstood and to contribute thoughts and ideas.

This book is only here because you are ....

Introduction

In an attempt to take people on a journey that they may not want to go on, I have said and heard it said many times by others, 'when we get things right for children in care, we can get things right for *all* children'. Following on from that, I almost always add 'when we learn from the adults that the children became, we are given a gift of wisdom from which to guide our work'. It is that very gift of wisdom that I will bring you in this book, the contents of which is underpinned by what I call the Triad of Knowledge; our lived experiences, our professional practice in the settings of social work and education and the academic research. This is a collective endeavour. The Triad is what we can collectively pull together but it is also what we bring individually; our own triad of knowledge. This knowledge, gained through what is termed Epistemology in academia (how do I know what I know in the world), is created by us all working together, listening to each other and bringing cultural humility into our work from the outset. We cannot know what we have not lived.

In this book you will notice that some chapters mostly draw on my academic experience and are heavily referenced and others on my practice in bringing about culture change through trauma-informed practices. In other chapters, you will hear a stronger personal voice, as if we were sitting together simply talking to one another and that will be a chapter drawing more on my lived experiences. In some instances, chapters are able to draw on the full Triad of Knowledge. We bring it all you see. We bring it all ….

DOI: 10.4324/9781003426592-1

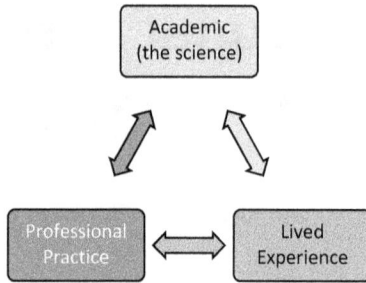

Figure I.1 The Triad of Knowledge

I have been immersed in the system of care, in relationship with the state, all my life. I have lived in it, worked in it and written about it for many years. Having first written in 1994 for my undergraduate dissertation about young people being isolated from a relational network and how this impacted self esteem, In 2013 I went on to write *The Brightness of Stars* about care-experienced adults, which was an attempt to provide alternative and nuanced narratives other than 'poor statistical outcomes' which was published by Routledge as a third edition in 2022. The third edition provided an opportunity to update the book and add new contemporary stories. As I read through the original chapters that I myself had written about my experiences, I recognised very quickly that I had healed in areas that were wounds in the first edition. This led me to think that the other original contributors must also have a different relationship with their texts. Apart from one person who I couldn't trace, all the writers offered a reflection providing a beautiful opportunity to present a book that demonstrated a healing journey, over time, in time.

In 2018, my MA in Education looked at the educational and employment trajectories of adults who were excluded from school. In 2021, Routledge published the award-winning book *Conversations That Make A Difference for Children and Young People* (Cherry, 2021) detailing how services, sectors and systems can work with children and young people from a trauma-informed perspective to increase relational practice and relational opportunities beyond services.

It is my hope that this book will guide you in weaving the web of belonging as well as enabling you to gain nuanced insights from my own research from which I drawhugely. My research asked the question 'How did care-experienced adults who were also excluded from school make sense of belonging?' and this book draws heavily on what was learnt. The presence of the participants is with you throughout, but it is in Chapter 3 that I shine the most powerful spotlight on their words so that you, the reader, can fully grasp how 'unbelonging' takes hold, right under our noses. It may be no surprise to you that it is regularly said to PhD students that nobody will *ever* read their thesis so it is very much my hope that this book will ensure that the rich findings that were gifted from that research will be made far more digestible, accessible and useful than it is in its current form within the academic space.

This book is divided into three parts. Part One creates the space for reflecting on and considering historical contexts; of ourselves in Chapter 1, of legislation in Chapter 2, of how stigma has infiltrated the discourse in Chapter 3 and, in Chapter 4, how 'unbelonging' is constructed and woven into the lives of children and young people facing multiple vulnerabilities. Part Two invites us to think about where we stand right now and what we can achieve with what we have. Chapter 6 argues the case for the deconstruction of the language used about children and young people. In Chapter 7, there is a call for us to view leadership as a collective responsibility and Chapter 8 asks us to look beyond what is in front of us and offers us a perspective on intersectionality. Finally, Part Three provides a conceptual framework to stimulate our thinking around how we can cultivate belonging in a team, a setting, a system and a service, then ends with what the implications of this wisdom are for policy, general practice and research. The book then closes with some final words.

Contrary to how services are set up and how we're invited to think about them, I take the view from the outset that education and children's services are inseparable. Children's lives are experienced holistically regardless of how different services and systems are demarcated, separated and constructed.

This book concentrates on children and young people facing marginalisation and disadvantages while focusing heavily on children in care. This focus sits alongside an understanding that these experiences are intersectional with lived experiences. Such experiences include being a person of colour in the UK, being a person with what are deemed additional educational needs, needs which go beyond the scope of what is considered 'normal' and are referred to as 'special needs', having neurodivergence and presenting behaviours that clearly signal distress referred to as social, emotional and mental health needs to name a few. Unpicking this paragraph alone would create several books, hence it is not within the scope of this one. However, when marginalisation and disadvantage are referred to, the reader is invited to visualise a child, a family, a community, in a holistic way, with multiple identities that are experienced in very particular ways. I ask that we collectively steer away from thinking about a child as simply a child in care, or a child with social emotional and mental health (SEMH) needs or an autistic child. We are complex and we live in a complex world.

The intersectionality outlined above is explored in Chapter 8 with the unashamed intention of demanding that research stop focusing on one aspect of a child or young person as if being 'in care' or being a 'black boy' or being 'a child with special educational needs' happens in isolation from the society in which we live or as though it is not experienced through current political agendas and specific legislation. To ignore intersectionality is to emulate the medical model which only seeks to look at the presenting 'issue' rather than looking at the whole picture. We can do better than that. We can be more sophisticated than that. More importantly, we need to be!

In many ways, and indeed, this was the attraction for myself; belonging offers us this opportunity to be holistic. Our human need to belong is universal and lifelong so the art of cultivating belonging is relevant for any setting, service or system. The principles are the same, the human motivation is the same, as is our capacity to create the conditions that make creating that sense of 'belonging' possible.

Weaving a Web of Belonging offers an original conceptual model and insight into cultivating belonging as an antidote to trauma. It raises the importance that all those working with children and young people have in considering the adult that the child will become, embedding practices that make the difference to those children and young people who rely on relationships, settings and communities. This book explores much of what is needed in order to deepen an understanding of the impact of trauma, inequity and marginalisation in services/education that further add to harm. In so doing, the reader is provided with a working conceptual model for culture change, cultivating belonging and making a difference to children and young people.

The need to belong is a fundamental and human motivation – a sense of fitting in or feeling like you are important in the context of something bigger, such as a family, a setting, a community – it is part of our internal drive. In my research, movement was the theme that consistently appeared across all the participants, across home, education settings and community. Where movement is unavoidable, such as for those children known to the social care system, unaccompanied asylum seekers and refugees, then belonging is essential. The Triad of Knowledge seeks to offer an accessible, informative and reflective read, with the child at the centre.

The final preparations of this book for publication coincide with a resurgence in thinking about belonging emerging in local authority strategic plans and vision, inspired by the recent Children's Social Care Review and Scotland's 'The Promise' (Scottish Government, 2020) which both, to varying degrees, highlight love. The embedding of trauma-informed frameworks in many services and settings has opened the door to deeper thinking about the 'how' of trauma-informed practice (to cultivate belonging) rather than the 'why' (do children and young people seek belonging in harmful places?), which supports making the notion of belonging a contemporary concern and an antidote to trauma.

Since 2010 many people have been soaking in the ideology of austerity. No group has felt this more than children and young people. As I write, there are nearly 4.3 million children living in poverty in the UK (Joseph Roundtree Foundation, 2024). The impact upon them has included punitive approaches to distress in schools, bottle-necked mental health services for children and young people with numbers rising, exponential numbers of children experiencing poorer mental health and wellbeing, the pandemic and its aftermath and a cost of living crisis which can more accurately be referred to as the Expansion of Poverty Crisis. If we are to mitigate some of the harms of the period since 2010, understanding our need to belong, and how belonging is cultivated, needs centralising in practice, in education settings, in social work practices and in settings where children in care live. Challenging the professional and societal stigmatisation of the experiences of being in care and of being excluded from school also needs active attention to reduce the self-stigma that children can then carry into adulthood. Finally, strategies employed to find belonging often result in more abuses of power, further stigmatisation and, often, system trauma. A deeper understanding of the lengths undertaken by those searching for belonging as those who need it most could result in more compassionate responses to distress and a desire for settings, services and systems to work in ways that understand the impact of movement, thus centralising the need to belong in practice, policy and legislation.

With all of this in mind, let's begin our weaving ….

References

Cherry, L. (2021). *Conversations That Make a Difference for Children and Young People: Relationship-focused Practice from the Front Line* (1st ed.). Abingdon: Routledge.

Cherry, L. (2022). *The Brightness of Stars; Stories from Care Experienced Adults to Inspire Change* (3rd ed.). Abingdon: Routledge.

Joseph Roundtree Foundation. (2024). *The Essential Guide to Understanding Poverty in the UK*. Retrieved on 22 July 2024 from https://www.jrf.org.uk/uk-poverty-2024-the-essential-guide-to-understanding-poverty-in-the-uk

Scottish Government (2020). *The Promise Scotland*. Retrieved on 9 May 2023 from https://thepromise.scot/about

PART ONE:
Weaving the Web of Belonging: The Historical Weaving of Unbelonging

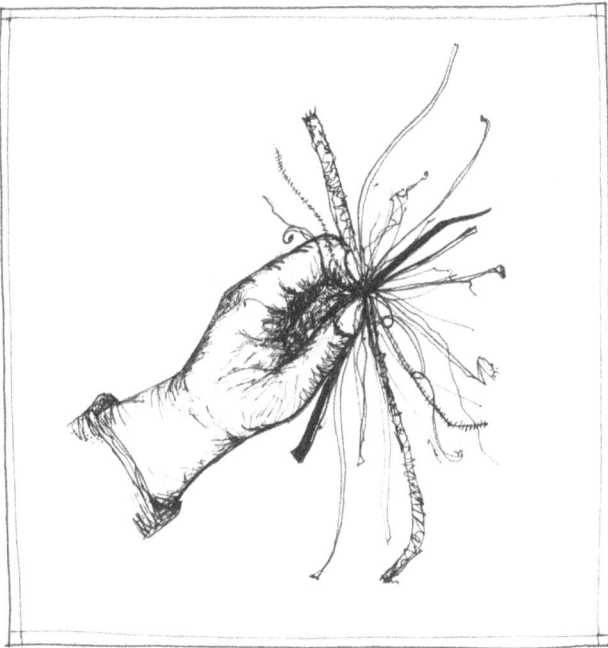

1

It Starts With Us

Introduction

Recognising and understanding who we are must always be the beginning, and this book starts with just that; where I am, what I bring and what I have, which is a reflection of my personal and professional history. We bring our own unique internal architecture, our 'wiring', much of which remains unseen. Therefore, in three bullet points, I start with myself so that you understand how the development of this book is inspired by three experiential aspects:

- My own journey through life and my ongoing relationship with finding a sense of belonging in different places and spaces at different times
- My own research at undergraduate, masters and doctoral levels
- Over 30 years of professional practice in social work settings, in education settings and in delivering learning and development and consultancy across the public sector.

If we are ever to embark on a trauma-informed journey then there really is no other place to start than with ourselves. Exploring our positionality (Jacobson and Mustafa, 2019) offers us a theoretical tool that asks us to consider what we bring to our work, to be conscious of who we are and what privileges we may have benefited from and in what areas of our lives we may have experienced marginalisation. I

DOI: 10.4324/9781003426592-3

therefore inform the reader that I arrive at the writing of this book as a white woman who is ostensibly middle class. I benefit from certain privileges: white privilege, colonial privilege and class privilege accentuated by undertaking my research in Oxbridge which is regarded as elitist (Bhopal and Alibhai-Brown, 2018).

That said, I have experienced marginalisation during my childhood and early adulthood through being raised by a single parent and my grandmother, by being in care in foster placements and children's homes in the 1980s and through experiencing the somewhat inevitable street homelessness at that time. However, I have lived much of my adult life from the position I have outlined above. My values, termed Axiology in academic spaces, argue that I cannot ask questions of others, for example in research, who belong to marginalised communities, even if they themselves are no longer marginalised, without seeking to create some change for those communities. It is my personal, professional and academic experience and positionality that has formed and shaped this view and you will undoubtedly see this expressed throughout my writing. Furthermore, it is from this position that I explore what counts as knowledge and who benefits from it and who/what it has the potential to transform (Edwards and Brannelly, 2017). It is important to me that my writing is not simply performative. I want … no! I demand change. I want to see change in service delivery, in social attitudes and in politics. The purpose of all of my work has to be for improvement.

My Relationship with Belonging

Entering the world in 1970, I experienced separation from my mother at birth in the mother and baby unit where I was born, which led to me entering my first foster placement. A few months after I was born, with adoption assumed, as it was for the children of unmarried mothers at that time, my grandmother decided and agreed that the baby, me, could be brought home. My childhood was spent with my gran and my mother as my mother lived at home with her mother, as opposed to any formal arrangement. I have never met my father and do not know his identity. My mother had a short marriage when I was 10 years old and when that broke down, we shared a flat, with my gran living across the road. However, as I started to enter adolescence, at around 12 years old, I went into care for the second time and never returned to my mother again. During this time, I was also excluded from two schools, attended an onsite education facility in a residential unit and spent some time in what would currently be termed Alternative Provision.

Being looked after away from home by the state is a unique experience for each individual in much the same way that family life is unique to each family. Furthermore, each of the children in that family can often describe very different versions of growing up with their parents. 'Care', in that regard, is no different. However being in care was an experience that has cast a long shadow. My experience of being in care was the ultimate exclusion, the most profound exclusion with my mother's words repeated throughout my childhood, 'Why can't you just fit in?' ringing in my ears for years to come. To then find myself unable to belong to a school community or a town, followed by experiencing homelessness after leaving care, which is not uncommon post care, the theme of belonging has persisted across my adult life.

School Exclusion and Belonging

After reflecting on school exclusion, what strikes me is that it is about so much more than being removed from a community. School exclusion is on a continuum with all of the other lived experiences the young person faced previously. It also directly relates to the experiences that will follow. It is about being removed from knowledge, from access to the next step in a learning journey and a removal from experiencing school belonging; belonging to the group of people who finished school, had a leaving event, a leaver's certificate and a basic foundation from formal education. It is the ultimate removal of factors that support and enable a sense of belonging, creating ruptures instead.

Education and Belonging

Reflecting across my life, I can see how much education has provided me with a sense of belonging, and I do not just mean the institutions that provide the bricks and mortar within which formal learning takes place. Having said that, a library will always make me swoon and a students' canteen with subsidised food will never fail to make me feel special. For me, it is the learning, the reading, the connections made between my experience of the world and academic accounts of how people make sense of the world they are living in. Reading lists excite me, presenting a whole new world for me to delve into. I undertook my first degree in Sociology in the early 1990s at the age of 21, just a few years later than my peers. With housing secured and the removal of legal and illegal substances from my body, I was very ready. Funded by a charity that supports young people who have been in care, I was able to take A levels and secure a place at Goldsmiths' College in London. The modules I chose, or maybe they chose me, were aligned with the life experiences that I needed to make sense of. As I explored 'The Sociology of Racism, of Feminism, of Identity and of Psychiatry', my first real breakthrough came with a reading list recommendation of *The Drama of Being a Child* (Miller, 1987). This book investigated the search for self from a psychotherapist's perspective, providing me with an opportunity to begin to explore who I was and how I was impacted by my own experiences.

My dissertation concerned the isolation experienced by coming out of care, and the impact upon a person's self-esteem. Several years later, I completed my MA in Education between 2016–2018 at Oxford Brookes University and chose to look at care experience, school exclusion and the employment and education trajectory across the life course. In order to do my MA, being without what were once known as 'O' levels, I had to take GCSEs in Maths and English and I also chose to do Biology, highlighting gaps in what might be termed 'general knowledge'. During my time at Oxford Brookes, I was invited to enter a Poster of my MA research in their 'Get Published' conference and received first prize for the 'Postgraduate Taught Highly Commended 2018 Award', which was an academic confidence boost. Now, again, I find myself back where I appear to belong; in education, cultivating decades of professional practice, academic learning and personal lived experiences into a document of research that can tell a story of how we search for and find belonging. It is also a picture of a lifetime's work, sharing the voices of those who cannot be heard however loud they may shout, reminding researchers that it is not about 'giving voice', rather it is working to ensure that those who write policy, develop legislation and deliver and create services listen to the voices that are already present.

Professional Experience and Belonging

It is strange that one might run out of the system of care with the speed of an athlete, going forwards, forwards, forwards and wanting to never look back, and then find oneself back in that system working professionally; yet many of us do just that. Between my first degree and my MA, my career was spent working in the fields of social work and education. For the first 20 years, I worked in the fields of Leaving Care Social Work, Education and Social Inclusion with young people and their families in a variety of roles, all of which were closely connected to care and to school exclusion. Working in and around exclusion and familial complexity gave rise to further curiosity about the nature of belonging and, of course, the question: did I belong in that profession? Particularly as I felt unable to be honest about my own experiences because of feelings of unsafety, of shame and stigma and of not having anyone I could discuss and share with. Since 2010 I have worked for myself, delivering training, speaking and writing on trauma, recovery and resilience, working with those doing the direct work rather than doing the direct work myself. Continuing to work in education and social work, my interest in how adults make sense of the experiences that happened in childhood has deepened (Cherry, 2021, 2022). This has culminated in the creation of an organisation called Trauma Informed Consultancy Services which I am very proud to lead.

Data or Wisdom

Throughout this book you will note references to 'data' and 'wisdom' and this is deliberate. In this chapter I have shared personal insights into various lived experiences which I gathered in my research. I felt strongly when I undertook my doctoral research that what I received was a gift, given through the generosity of people's personal stories and insights into their own experiences. I felt that to consider these gifts as 'data' gave academic rigour to my work but that the language of academia took away the depth of what was gifted to me from the participants. I was convinced that they offered wisdom, a wisdom so often ignored, silenced and misunderstood. In fact, it is a wisdom that is rarely asked for in academic literature and this book is a tool providing the depth that the participants who selflessly gifted me their time to share their experiences deserve. The collective hope is that this book will assist more practitioners to consider their role in supporting others to make sense of their belonging.

Summary

I entered the research and now this book, knowing that I am deeply tangled up in the process; the research question and the methods that I chose are not outside of me. This book's focus, layout and title are shaped from my life experiences. I am in and of a process that has no beginning and no end. I arrive at this work challenging various ideas about who controls and owns research and what knowledge is valid. Settings, services and systems can lead cultural change in how services can be deconstructed so that the focus is on cultivating belonging through the evaluation of language that problematise the person outside of context, through an understanding of stigma that demands the removal of it and through transformational leadership. I am within it, of it, underneath it and looking in on it. It is, because I am, because we are ... that this book exists. In Chapter 2 we go on a historical journey of the underpinning legislation, the soundtrack to children who come into contact with the state.

Key Chapter Takeaways

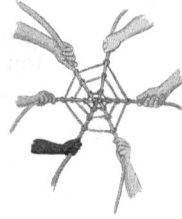

- We cannot separate ourselves from our own experiences. Self-awareness is key to curiosity.

- Belonging is a backdrop to all of our lives, its presence is dependent upon how we have experienced it.

Reflection

Some lives are a journey, others an expedition. I started this chapter inviting us to consider the idea that we start with where we are, with what we bring and with what we have. Please take a moment to consider where you are, what experiences and ways of viewing the world you have and what you have available to you as resources at this time of your life. This reflection is an ongoing one across different times of our lives and it is my hope that you will revisit this personal enquiry regularly.

References

Bhopal, K. and Alibhai-Brown, Y. (2018). *White Privilege: The Myth of a Post-racial Society*. Bristol and Chicago, IL: Policy Press.

Cherry, L. (2021). *Conversations That Make a Difference: Relationship-focused Practice from the Front Line* (1st ed.). Abingdon: Routledge. https://doi.org/10.4324/9781003124375

Cherry, L. (2022). *The Brightness of Stars; Stories from Care Experienced Adults to Inspire Change* (3rd ed.). Abingdon: Routledge.

Edwards, R. & Brannelly, T. (2017). Approaches to democratising qualitative research methods. *Qualitative Research,* 17(3): 271–277.

Jacobson, D., & Mustafa, N. (2019). Social identity map: a reflexivity tool for practicing explicit positionality in critical qualitative research. *International Journal of Qualitative Methods,* 18: 160940691987007.

Miller, A. (1987). *The Drama of Being a Child: The Search for the True Self.* London: Virago.

2

Carrying the Burden of the Past

Introduction

In Chapter 1, I have attempted to contextualise my experiences for the reader and explored my arrival at the place I find myself writing this book. Now it's time to turn to the broad historical context that lies behind where we stand today. If we are to understand belonging using a wider lens than our own experiences, then we must first understand 'unbelonging' and the very deliberate historical context of it. It is in this vein that this chapter explores the historical context of children in care and education. This history requires some exploration, together with the relevant legislation and policy, alongside the administrative data, which provides this opportunity.

Historical Exploration

This is a somewhat overwhelming task due to the vast amount of law and policy to navigate and it can be a lot to untangle, as the relationships that existed between child welfare and education were not well developed for lengthy periods. But I urge you to bear with me. This historical chapter won't be everyone's cup of tea, but it is necessary because it situates children, children in care and their education within the social and political contexts, across the decades. This undertaking also ensures that there is a recognition of children as being vulnerable. Furthermore, their need for rights has been centuries in the making; all children have a right to education and to protection, and marginalised and disadvantaged children and families have a right to be interwoven into child protection. This exploration is designed to help further understanding about how those with experiences of having been in care have an intergenerational history which can often disappear from the contemporary challenges that are faced in this arena.

I am clear that the history of the treatment of children in need of care is pertinent to understanding some of the challenges currently faced by those children who are living in care, those known to a social worker and those who face various external vulnerabilities such as poverty and racism, for example, or disabilities and neurodivergences. This long history creates an important perspective on children and young people and how it might manifest itself across the life course in relation to their sense of belonging.

Legislation

The first piece of legislation that allowed the state to intervene and permanently transfer guardianship of a child from parents to a third party was the Act for the Care and Education of Infants Who May Be Convicted of Felony 1840. Ward explains how:

> In the 1880s legislation was introduced through which natural parents could permanently forfeit the custody of their children to third parties. The Prevention of Cruelty to and Protection of Children Act 1889 was introduced to separate children from parents who were considered unfit; the Poor Law Amendment Act 1889, the Custody of Children Act 1891 and the Industrial Schools Act 1891 prevented certain children who had already been cared

for by the state or the voluntary societies from returning to their parents. The legislation formed the basis for a number of procedures which were used to regulate the relationship between natural parents, children and child care organisations for the next century.

(1990, p. 43)

However, previous legislation had already made the situation difficult for these children. The Poor Law Amendment Act 1834 aimed to reduce dependency on the state and ensure that the poor were housed and fed in the workhouse. As wages were so inadequate, it was virtually impossible to provide a lower standard of poor relief without widespread starvation. The solution was to perceive dependency on the state as a moral failing and to stigmatise paupers. Most children in care were pauper children with the voluntary societies taking in far fewer children than the statutory authorities, and some only taking in legitimate children of a 'better class'. Illegitimate children, who were overrepresented in pauper establishments, were further stigmatised, as were children with disabilities. This deliberate stigmatisation of pauper children in the 19th century produced a legacy that has been hard to eradicate.

The beginning of the expansion of central government in the 19th century led to the shift in the oversight of children's welfare, making it a legal requirement to protect children (Jones, 2010). Between 1885 and 1913, no less than 52 Acts of Parliament affecting child welfare were passed (Boushel et al., 2000) reflecting changing attitudes towards children over that time. It is not possible to write about children's welfare without also considering the treatment of their mothers, as this is where the story of children in care often begins. The Foundling Hospital was founded in 1739 by Thomas Coram, as a place for saving poor parents from shame, poverty and infanticide, but with an emphasis on the poor unwanted child rather than on the mother (Williams, 2018). Workhouses were particularly aimed at poor, destitute and unmarried mothers and intended to be seen as a deterrent while also providing a place for childbirth (Williams, 2018). However, the hospital was opened as a result of Coram seeing so many dead babies on the streets of London. It provided a place where a mother could leave her infant believing it would be cared for. Children were given a new name on arrival and the mother was given a token so that in the rare circumstance that she should find herself in a tenable position to return for her child the child could be identified. The new name had no connection with anyone with whom the child came into contact and the new birth certificate that they were given until 1953 labelled them as coming from the Foundling Hospital, indicating that they were foundlings. The museum stands there to this day displaying all the things that the mothers left with their 'abandoned' babies. Illegitimacy was a huge issue of a magnitude that is hard to imagine in contemporary times, it was assumed that unmarried mothers would want to hide their sin through killing their infant; they were blamed for being poor, blamed for betraying the father of the child, stigmatised and deemed a burden (Higginbotham, 2017). The child of an unmarried mother could be harshly described: 'The bastard, like the prostitute, thief and beggar, belongs to that motley crowd of disreputable social types which society has generally resented, always endured. He is a living symbol of social irregularity' (Davis, 1939). Having a child outside marriage was considered to be an offence against the sacrament of matrimony, and a threat to the good order of society, right up until the mid-20th century. An illegitimate child was described as *filius nullius*, nobody's child.

Theoretically an illegitimate child had no legal relations. Illegitimate children, who were overrepresented in the care system, were actively and deliberately stigmatised. Arguably, this historical legacy of the stigmatisation of children in care is one of the reasons why children in care continue to be stigmatised. In addition, there was the deliberate stigmatisation of paupers and their children following the 1834 Poor Law, where shame and stigma were actively attributed as this was seen as a deterrent. It was no accident that these children were deliberately made to feel that they did not belong, that they should feel ashamed and would be stigmatised by society. This ancestral and historical legacy has yet to be overcome. It can be observed within policy and

Table 2.1   Table of Early Legislation Regarding the Welfare of Children

The Poor Law Amendment Act 1834
Act for the Care and Education of Infants Who May Be Convicted of Felony 1840
The Prevention of Cruelty to and Protection of Children Act 1889
The Poor Law Amendment Act 1889
The Custody of Children Act 1891
The Industrial Schools Act 1891

legislation across the centuries, highlighting to what public attitudes towards the family, social justice, the deserving and undeserving poor, women and ideas about mothering can be attributed.

Unbelonging

As noted above, there were active mechanisms in place to ensure 'unbelonging', focusing on unmarried mothers, their children and 'the poor'. An illegitimate child belonged to no-one and there was an active endeavour to ensure that a child in care no longer belonged to their families.

Unbelonging and stigma are inextricably linked and are very much a legacy that is embedded in current legislation and practice. Belonging is a relatively recent concept that can be more closely associated with Bowlby's Attachment Theory (1944) than with anything that came before it. There is also evidence that, just as the Foundling Hospital children never saw any sentimental items their parents had left with them when they were admitted, children in care today often lose sight of personal items such as photographs and jewellery that symbolise a connection with their past and may reinforce a sense of belonging (Ward, 2021).

If positive practices of belonging are absent from the history of social care, we should now turn to consider its place in the history of education. Education and children's social care legislation regarding the protection of children intertwine and serve to highlight the inter-connected nature of care and education in children's experience; this legislation was initially born out of notions about destitute children and work and, later on, basic education as preparation for work.

Education and Children's Social Care

During the 18th century when there were no rights or laws in place to offer children any protection, they often died young and were treated with brutality; there was little understanding of children as developing humans. As the 19th century concluded, much had moved on: health and sanitation had improved, children were less likely to be found work-ing under the age of 12 years old and there was a better understanding of the concept of childhood (Hopkins, 1994). Mary Carpenter played a significant role in the development of industrial schools established for the 'perishing classes'; destitute children who had not yet offended but were thought likely to do so were sent to them with the objective of deflecting them from crime. Underpinned by Christianity, Carpenter's mission was 'to carry education to the lowest depths of society, to seek out in their hiding-places the most wretched and deserted children ... to raise them from their hopeless condition' (Carpenter, 1851, p. 110). They were called 'ragged schools', it seems, because the children were thought to be ragged and filthy and so the schools provided not only education but also clothes and food for the poor. One of the original aims of the ragged schools was to provide food for the poor, whereas the gap in educational attainment had been narrowing.

The various Industrial Schools Acts (1857–1881) defined the grounds on which children could be committed to the care of the state, regard-less of the wishes of their parents. These grounds and others intro-duced by legislation such as the Prevention of Cruelty to Children Act 1889, formed the basis for separating children from their birth families through fit person orders, and later care orders, until the implementa-tion of the Children Act 1989.

However, only a relatively small proportion of children in care were placed in industrial schools or, as they became later known, community homes with education (CHEs). The majority of children looked after by the state were placed in workhouses, poor law schools, foster homes or residential homes and foster care from the mid-20th century onwards. The education of pauper children in general is where some ambivalence can be found. If they were not educated, they were unlikely to achieve independence in adulthood and would therefore remain a burden on the state, but if they were educated, until universal education was introduced, they would have an advantage that was not open to the children of the independent labourer. This created a conundrum regarding the education of children in care, arguably a legacy that remained across the centuries until intentional mechanisms were put in place, that is explored further in this section.

Finally, there was the concern that educating these children would cause them to no longer be satisfied with their situation in life. Children in the care of the statutory authorities and the larger voluntary societies had better opportunities for education than their peers in the 19th century and in the early years of the 20th century. However, as universal education opened up greater opportunities, this advantage was gradually lost. The need to reduce dependency on the state meant that some were denied access to secondary education because it was thought imperative that they stop being a burden on the state as soon as possible. This legacy of ambivalence is one of the factors that lies behind persistently low aspirations for looked-after children.

For children with additional needs, the Elementary Education (Blind and Deaf Children) Act of 1893 extended compulsory education to include blind and deaf children, establishing special schools, and, six years later, provision was made for physically impaired children in the Elementary Education (Defective and Epileptic Children) Act of 1899 (UK Parliament, 1899).

Furthermore, in a bid to ensure that children were healthier, further assistance under the Education (Provision of Meals) Act in 1906 allowed local authorities to provide free school meals, later extended and made compulsory by the Education Act 1944 (UK Parliament, 1944). These shifts in attitudes show the beginning of the infusion of the education and welfare of children in legislation.

Let's Take A Moment …

Before we move into more contemporary leg-islation, I want to acknowledge that the first part of this chapter is a lot! When I share the historical contexts of legislation in keynotes, around a third of the room sit up with excitement, another third slump down in despair and the remainder of the group have nodded off. That said, in order to understand where we are today, we really do need to understand where we've been.

Whichever group you are in, it's time to move the body, not least because we want to move forward, not get too exasper-ated by the past. We can understand the past without having to move back to it. We're visitors to the past. So please take some time to move; stand up and sit down seven times in the chair you're in, or go for a walk, or stand barefoot in the garden, run up and down the stairs three times, or if you need to stay seated, move whatever part of your body moves. Just move and then when you return to this next section, you will be well and truly grounded into the present.

Recent Legislation

This brings us up to date. The Children Act 1989 swept away the grounds for children coming into care for reasons that had persisted since the 19th century, such as illegitimacy and poverty and replaced them with the criteria that the child is suffering or is likely to suffer significant harm. The Act reframes the relationship between the state and the family specifying (Section 17) that the state has a duty to promote the welfare of children in their area who are in need, and to provide services designed to ensure that children achieve or have the opportunity to achieve a reasonable standard of health and development. This child development perspective formed the basis for the policies introduced by the Labour governments of 1997–2010.

In 1991 the UK ratified the UN Convention on the Rights of the Child (UNCRC) which provided a statement of children's rights with four guiding principles: Non-discrimination (Article 2), Best interest of the child (Article 3), Right to life survival and development (Article 6) and the Right to be heard (Article 12) (Unicef, 1990). The latter is a landmark in the history of children who had previously been understood as voiceless. This shift to the idea that children have rights can be seen in the legislation that followed such as the Protection of Children Act 1999, which made it a legal requirement for a list to be kept of all those unsuitable to work with children because they had harmed a child or placed a child at harm. Articles 24 and 28 of the Rights of Persons with Disabilities also state the right of disabled people to receive an education. Having been given the right to participate in education in 1970, it was only with the ratification of the Equality Act 2010 that disabled people were protected from discrimination in the UK, including in education.

Policy on children in care has moved between various government departments, such as the Home Office to the Department of Health, to the Department for Children, Schools and Families (DfES) in 2007. It was under New Labour (1997–2010) that several policies and legislation that directly impacted children and young people in care was ushered in. Many reforms that impacted children in care were introduced such as Education Action Zones, established by the Secretary of State for Education and Employment in 1998–1999 under the School Standards and Framework Act 1998. These zones were introduced to raise educational standards for those children and young people in seriously disadvantaged areas, however they were not deemed a great success and were discontinued (Reid and Brain, 2003). The Every Child Matters policy agenda, launched partly in response to the death of 8-year-old Victoria Climbie, focused on a number of identified outcomes that all children's services had to work towards with the objective of improving the lives of children and narrowing the gap between the most disadvantaged and their peers (DfES, 2003).

The Care Matters White Paper (DfES, 2007) was particularly pertinent in relation to the education of looked-after children. This focus on children and young people in care together with those in the most disadvantaged areas created a culture of placing children at the heart of care and education. This shift in focus went on to pave the way for increased attention to ensuring foster carers supported education, as evidenced by the guidance under Section 20 of the Children and Young Persons Act 2008. This required the development of designated teachers (DTs), the introduction in 2011 by the Coalition Government of Personal Education Plans (PEPs) legislated in Section 36 of the 2008 Act. This was followed by the role of virtual school headteachers (VSHs) becoming statutory in the Children and Families Act 2014, together with Education, Health and Care Plans (EHCPs).

The sole purpose of virtual schools is to oversee the education of children in care by driving up the performance of schools in relation to these children, providing local authorities with the power to enforce this. These powers included directing schools to admit children in care, even where the school is fully subscribed, and developing better support in schools to prevent exclusions of children in care (DfES, 2007). There was also now an understanding that children in care were ten times more likely to be excluded from school than their peers (SEU, 1998). After a pilot of the service, virtual schools became a statutory service directed by the Children and Families Act 2014. These have had much success and an impact has been had on reducing the numbers of exclusions for children in care (DfE, 2019). So successful has the virtual school approach been that its reach was extended through the

Children and Social Work Act 2017 to previously looked-after children (those who have been adopted) and guidance released from the DfE (2021) extended support to all children with a social worker.

An evaluation of this extension is being undertaken by the Rees Centre at the University of Oxford. The question remains as to whether the reduction of the number of children in care being excluded has in fact gone down, or whether the use of off-rolling, managed moves and fixed-term exclusions have increased, making calculating the actual numbers impossible.

Recognition that Section 24 of the Children Act 1989 needed to extend to offer a better package of care was legislated in the Children (Leaving Care) Act 2000. This replaced Section 24 in a bid to make the duties and responsibilities of local authorities towards those young people who had been in their care a legal requirement. Further duties were introduced including that young people coming out of care should be better prepared to live on their own and that a Personal Advisor should be allocated to each young person to provide support. A further introduction was that the Personal Advisor must provide a Pathway Plan for any child for whom they are responsible. While there

Table 2.2   Recent Legislation and Policy

Children Act 1989
UN Convention on the Rights of the Child ratified in the UK in 1991
Protection of Children Act 1999
Care Standards Act 2000
Children (Leaving Care) Act 2000
Every Child Matters policy agenda (2003)
Children Act 2004
Care Matters White Paper (2007)
Children and Young Person's Act 2008
Children and Families Act 2014
Children and Social Work Act 2017

were criticisms that the Act did not go far enough (Grover et al., 2004), the shift in trajectory cannot be understated.

Regional differences across the home nations began to emerge. Around the same time the Children's Commissioner for Wales Act 2001 created the first children's commissioner post in the UK, whose principal aim was to safeguard and promote the rights and welfare of children. Northern Ireland followed next (Commissioner for Children and Young People (NI) Order 2003), then Scotland (Commissioner for Children and Young People (Scotland) Act 2003) and finally England (Sections 1–9 of the Children Act 2004). The Education Act 2002, specified the requirement for school governing bodies and further education (FE) institutions to safeguard and promote the welfare of children.

Summary

The period of New Labour could easily be argued to have provided a holistic approach to thinking about children in care and education. The DfES was renamed the Department for Education (DfE) in 2010 by the incoming Coalition Government, in response to a view that the focus had shifted too much to welfare and not enough on education. The Every Child Matters policies ended, re-establishing the tension between education and welfare.

The trajectory, through the lens of policy and legislation, demonstrates not just how much things have changed, but also what has not changed. The historical relationship between poverty and care, care and education, class and care, stigmatisation and the movement towards children's rights can be followed in the legislation. Governments, in theory, identify a problem, gather information and research, produce a policy, conduct an impact assessment and then draft legislation and statutory guidance to implement it. This directly impacts children's and young people's experiences of those sectors. Policy is implemented and interpreted into practice delivery. Research can feed into all of these areas and activism plays a role in leading change from the ground up. However, these processes are often framed by the law and language of the past. Chapter 3 helps us understand how the past is never far away when it comes to children and young people who are in contact with the state.

***

Key Chapter Takeaways

- Understanding and making explicit the history of unbelonging, stigma and shame in relation to certain children and the relationship in policy between education and children's services helps us determine where we can start to weave in belonging.
- Services are set up in ways that separate different aspects of children's lives, but this is not how children live. For example, children with a social worker, especially children who are in care, are not separate from the other services they may access.
- Overall, belonging is missing from this children's policy landscape; indeed historically unbelonging was the implicit aim of policy and law. Ultimately, children continue to be at the mercy of government ideology, social attitudes and socio-economic resources.

Reflection

Where can unbelonging be seen in my setting? Is it in the language we use? Is it in the values, beliefs or attitudes of others? After deep reflection, what values, attitudes or beliefs do I hold that contribute to 'unbelonging' culturally? When have I experienced unbelonging? How did it make me feel? What brought me back to a place of feeling belonging?

References and Bibliography

Boushel, M., Fawcett, M., & Selwyn, J. (2000). *Focus on Early Childhood: Principles and Realities*. Oxford: Blackwell Science.

Bowlby, J. (1944). Forty-four juvenile thieves: their characters and home-life (II). *International Journal of Psychoanalysis*, 25: 107–128.

Carpenter, M. (1851). Evening ragged schools. In *Reformatory Schools*. Cambridge: Cambridge University Press.

Davis, K. (1939). Illegitimacy and the social structure. *The American Journal of Sociology*, 45(2): 215–233.

Department for Education (DfE). (2019). School exclusion: a literature review on the continued disproportionate exclusion of certain children. Retrieved 22 June 2021 from https://assets.publishing.service.gov.uk/government/ uploads/system/uploads/attachment_data /file/800028/Timpson_review _of_school_exclusion_literature_review.pdf

Department for Education (DfE). (2021). Children looked after in England including adoptions. Retrieved 27 June 2022 from https://explore -education-statistics.service.gov.uk/find-statistics/children-looked-after-in -england-including-adoptions/2021

DfES (Department for Education and Skills (DfES). (2003). Every Child Matters. Green Paper, Cm. 5860. London: The Stationery Office (TSO).

Department for Education and Skills (DfES). (2007). Care Matters. UK Parliament Command Paper. Retrieved 23 June 2021 from https:// assets.publishing.service.gov.uk/government/uploads/system/uploads/ attachment_data /file/326311/Care_Matters_-_Time_for_Change.pdf

Grover, C. G., Stewart, J. M., & Broadhurst, K. (2004). Transitions to adulthood: some critical observations of the Children (Leaving Care) Act 2000. *Social Work and Social Sciences Review*, 11(1): 5–18.

Higginbotham, P. (2017). *Children's Homes: A History of Institutional Care for Britain's Young*. Pen & Sword History.

Hopkins, E. (1994). *Childhood Transformed: Working-class Children in Nineteenth-century England*. Manchester: Manchester University Press.

Jones, R. (2010). Children Acts 1948–2008: the drivers for legislative change in England over 60 years. *Journal of Children's Services*, 4(4): 39–52.

Reid, I., & Brain, K. (2003). Education action zones: mission impossible? *International Studies in Sociology of Education*, 13(2): 195–216.

Social Exclusion Unit (SEU). (1998). Truancy and school exclusion. Retrieved on 16 June 2021 from https://dera.ioe.ac.uk/5074/2/D5074New.pdf

Unicef (1990) Convention on the Rights of the Child (1989) Treaty no. 27531. United Nations Treaty Series, 1577, pp. 3-178. Retrieved 3 July 2022 from https://treaties.un.org/doc/Treaties/1990/09/19900902%2003-14%20AM/Ch_IV_11p.pdf

United Nations (UN). (1999). UN Convention on the Rights of the Child (UNCRC). Retrieved on 23 July 2024 from https://www.unicef.org.uk/wp-content/uploads/2016/08/unicef-convention-rights-child-uncrc.pdf

Ward, H. (1990). The charitable relationship: parents, children and the waifs and strays society. PhD dissertation, University of Bristol.

Ward, H. (2021). Transitions to adulthood from care in late 19th century England. *Child and Family Social Work*, 26(2): 222–230.

Williams, S. (2018). *Unmarried Motherhood in the Metropolis, 1700–1850: Pregnancy, the Poor Law and Provision* (1st ed.). Cham, Switzerland: Springer International Publishing.

3

The Stigma Wound

Introduction

Stigmatisation experienced by children in care is forever present, even if we don't talk about it. It is a wound and wounds can linger if not given the right conditions to heal. Stigma was one of the themes that emerged from my research and yet the word itself was not referred to even once! However, t permeated throughout. In my work around the country, I hear young people who are in care or are leaving that system talk about stigma and shame all the time. This provides testament to the unwelcome reality that not only has time failed to reduce stigma, it is in fact an ancestral wound, arguably a hangover of the historical context as laid out in Chapter 2. It is weaved into the experience, just as it was all those centuries ago and we have yet to unpick, unthread, rethread and reweave alternative narratives and understandings of experiences.

Much has been written about stigma, building on Goffman's seminal work which defined stigma as a social process that was discrediting to individuals and groups based on a perception of difference that affected the way a person was seen as a whole (Goffman, 1963). Goffman considered that types of stigma came about because of mental illness, physical disabilities and identification with a particular race, ethnicity or religion, which have taken place. This focus on particular characteristics that are fixed and distinct, based on the idea that there is a 'norm', has created much interest in the study of stigma. A

DOI: 10.4324/9781003426592-5

multi-disciplinary interest has given rise to a debate over the definition (Link and Phelan, 2001) and a rejection of the term by those with lived experiences (Pescosolido and Martin (2015) has dominated the discourse. After being taken apart within many contexts, disciplines and accounts of experiences, stigma is now more broadly understood as a social process (Manago et al., 2022) or as the 'machinery of inequality' (Tyler, 2020, p. 1).

Stigmatisation disrupts belonging, not least because it is so often silenced, misunderstood and avoided. If we don't talk about it, then we don't know it's there, right? Wrong! There are three aspects to stigmatisation that I want to highlight; professional stigma, social stigma and self stigma. In this chapter, I will explore these, arguing that self stigma is a wound derived from professional and social stigma. Furthermore, I'll put forward the view that stigma, trauma and power all work together, relying on various mechanisms that make it difficult to talk about one without the other. I will do this by drawing extensively from my research.

Research Themes

There were nine themes that came through in the research as shown in Figure 3.1.

Stigma and Movement

Although stigma was not mentioned, movement was talked about by every single participant demonstrating that for a child in care movement is unavoidable; movement of relationships, of homes, of education settings, of communities, of pets, of bedrooms. Knowing this makes weaving belonging into practice as a tool for healing trauma

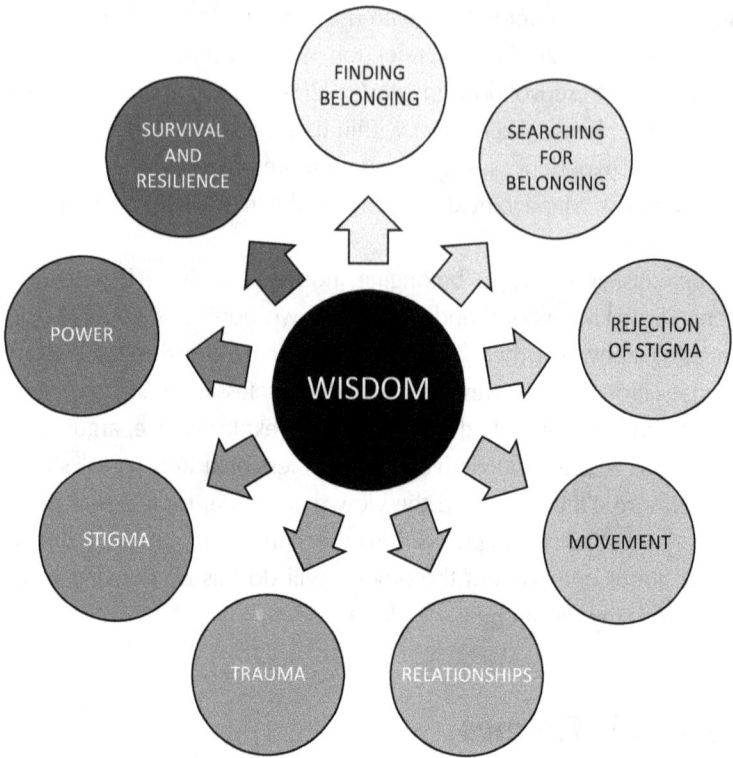

Figure 3.1 Research Themes

an essential aspect of practice. Within that experience of movement came the internal interpretations as to why the movement happened, and it also brought to the fore numerous strategies to enable children to survive and adapt to those situations.

> I was passed around quite a lot... so I was passed down through their family first and then the care system. ... like you know 'cause you're like, part of like your travel.
>
> (Shaun)

Below Jenny shares an internal interpretation when she talks about the sensation of feeling as though she was 'getting lost in the system' having moved around different places they lived, including countries.

> *So it started off in coming to the UK and then when I got to 11, I went back to (another country) and then when I'm there, I was gonna come back for secondary school to the UK but then my mum's mental health deteriorated. I was taken into care for bits of that and got placed back with my mum and then I was from the ages of kind of 14 upwards I was exploited. So then I was in care kind of 16 to 17, but then I've got to that age where they don't know what to do with you. And then yeah, kind of got lost in the system on there onwards.*
>
> (Jenny)

The movement between education settings is further observed by Maisie.

> *By the time I was 12 I'd already been to three mainstream primary schools. I was excluded when I was eight and then the next one. I went for a year and a half and they excluded me again and I went to a behaviour school and I did really well there like small classes with two teachers. You had to do certain amounts and then like we had like a morning break in afternoon break and then lunch. So it was quite separated. I did really well there, so they moved me back to a mainstream school.*
>
> (Maisie)

The implication of doing 'really well' in what Maisie describes as a 'behaviour school' created more movement as she explains below.

> *I struggled back in mainstream education again because I was different to those kids. You know, I just wasn't... we weren't the same and I struggled with the setting. I struggled with everything. I was excluded a lot, didn't go to classes. I liked PE and I'd always been a keen footballer but I wasn't allowed to do PE. I eventually got expelled from there.*
>
> (Maisie)

An unintended consequence of the success of the alternative provision was the return to mainstream. In doing well in an alternative provision, Maisie was then returned to a mainstream school which she was unable to cope with, causing more exclusions and more educational and home movement.

In the following excerpt, Crystal shares some of the reasons for movement that might not be talked about normally, and also demonstrates how the complexity of the 'system' fuses with the child and their sense of moving from place to place. The idea that a child is 'lucky' to be fostered rather than placed in residential care is remembered alongside the types of experiences that one might have when living in a setting with other children who are also in care. For example, the almost incidental way that a resident ending their life by suicide is mentioned suggests that many very difficult things happen that are just part of the experience. Furthermore, it is in the context of this tragic event that another move is required.

> *First off, I was put in a children's home. Actually, they're like assessment units, so I was there for about probably about 3 months, then they said to me, because you're quite a well-behaved child we will try and get you a*

foster carer ... you're really lucky because most teenag-
ers don't go into foster care so I went in to an awful foster
carers for about 6 weeks and she was much more awful
to my younger foster brother than me and then thank-
fully she gave up fostering. Then I went into the worst
children's home in the town which everyone at the time
in care went. Then I went to another children's home
after one of the residents killed himself, then I went to
the children's home in the town that was for longer-
term children. I then went back to the other children's
home and then I went into a semi-secure setting, when
my case was going through Criminal Court. I went from
there to another foster placement, then back to that unit
again, then to another children's home and then back to
that unit again where I stayed until I was 18.

(Crystal)

The way that Crystal talks about suicide, about her 'case' going through
a criminal court and the endless moves provokes either a sense of
detachment to such debilitating experiences or a sense of integration
and 'normalised' experiences reveals how movement brings to the
fore so many different experiences. She describes a children's home,
which is a home where a group of children and young people live and
are looked after by paid staff. She then describes it as a 'unit' rather
than a home suggesting more of a coldness towards the setting as the
memory comes to the fore. The assessment she speaks of leaves her
with very clear feelings about being assessed as to whether she was
'good' and therefore allowed to leave and go to a foster placement.
A foster placement is a family configuration where a child who is in
care can be looked after as part of that family. Crystal highlights here
the way in which a foster home is thought of as a 'good' home to be
in unlike a children's home which is where you might get sent if you
are not 'good'. It is not the place of this research to address the complex discussion around residential homes and foster homes and the

nuanced debate that has always been present on where children are best placed: in total, 11 different home moves are described in this quote.

However, what is clear is that Crystal has internalised this debate as a child and has felt the unspoken and spoken views of the adults around her. She has experienced the stigmatisation of being in care, understood the stigma of different types of care and carried that into adulthood.

Additionally, other recollections of movement demonstrate the vulnerability and fragility of complex family relationships around formal care provision.

> I moved around quite a lot when I was younger, so I always lived in foster placements or with ... I lived with a lot of friends when I was younger as well because I was just very unsettled. My dad still had parental rights, so he would be able to bring me back in and out of care and it was never challenged so I often slept on the streets because when my step mum would come home, who had quite severe mental health problems, she didn't want me there. So my dad would then kick me out and that happened the first time I think I was eight. So from the age of eight until I got my own place, when I was 16 ... I've never lived in any hostels or any residential homes or anything like that. I've always lived with friends, family and foster carers.
>
> (Alisha)

The movement described by Alisha is of foster placements, friends and moving in and out of care and home. She talks of feeling unwanted at home but does not talk about feeling wanted in any of the other settings. My sense making here leaves me curious about whether finding belonging in endless moves in care is less important than feeling a sense of belonging in the home.

The internalisation of the reasons for the movement are demonstrated by Shaun as he has developed the view that he is a 'problem child'.

> *I went into a children's home and that was the worst time of my life ... it was bad things happening ... really bad things happened ... it was terrible. They moved me from place to place ... problem child. Nobody can control me 'cause I won't get medicated. Nobody had the time to take me to the doctors and medicate me. So I was living with an illness which I didn't know about.*
>
> (Shaun)

Movement had an impact on his health, on his ability to get to appointments, on being somewhere long enough to receive a diagnosis, on being somewhere long enough for any professional to develop a curiosity behind the behaviour rather than medicate the behaviour. In this quote, we hear how Shaun has internalised the idea that he is a 'problem child', he has taken on that label. He cannot 'control' himself and no-one can 'control' him. He also shares the unspeakable but does not speak about whatever the 'terrible things' were that happened to him.

Types of Movement

All those who took part in my research talked about movement; movement between home settings such as foster placements, children's homes, back and forth between their family home and care settings, prison settings and secure settings. Movement was also talked about geographically around the UK and, for some, between countries. Equally, movement between education settings was spoken of by them all. Every move offered an opportunity for a new relationship that might make a difference, for a sense of belonging, for safety from trauma. However, what is mainly described is how movement was a thread, a thread entrenched in power, stigma and trauma. This power was expressed through how it is decided where the child goes, trauma was expressed by what happened to the child once they arrived somewhere, and stigma was expressed by the way the experience was stigmatised by society and other professionals.

A child has little, if any, power over where they live and where they might receive education. For children in care, this lack of power is amplified by all the experiences that have preceded it. For example, Donna speaks of the process of being moved, but also of having another person pack her belongings,

> We had our bags packed for us and moved elsewhere and moved to the next place.
>
> (Donna)

The implication here is that the packing was done by someone with whom they had no meaningful relationship, who went through their things and packed them. There is a history of children in care's belongings being packed and moved in bin bags, something which has been ardently campaigned against for decades. We can see that children who have been in care experiencing stigmatisation is not a new phenomenon, as previously suggested, and that it can arguably be attributed to the long shadow cast by early recorded care experiences of the 19th century.

In the research, the word 'stigma' showed up as not being good enough, not being acceptable, and was clearly identifiable throughout the research as a shared and implicit narrative emerging from participants' descriptions and reflections.

In describing themselves and their views of themselves, participants referred to feelings from childhood while also sharing current reflections and assumptions.

> I was a problem child.
>
> (Maisie)

Additionally, Sam, a 50-year-old, mixed-race woman, spoke of the intersection between racism and classism.

> *I was bullied for being mixed race after I moved to a pre-dominantly white area council estate. I would explore any way I could to become 'white' like them, I put talc on my face, hated my dad for being Indian, tried to dress like my peers but couldn't always afford it.*
>
> (Sam)

The description 'a predominantly white area council estate' suggests that she believes us to share an implicit understanding of that to mean 'working class'. In her descriptions, she expresses what being mixed race in a 'predominantly white area council estate' was like to experience.

As a 28-year-old white woman and social work graduate, Alisha also talks about her 'negative beliefs' and a sense of not being good enough.

> *So I have to reinvent myself and I have to recreate myself and teach myself who the person I am is and who I want to be and you know, try and challenge myself all the time on these negative beliefs I have about myself and it's fucking hard work.*
>
> (Alisha)

This internal narrative, describing negative beliefs, suggests that she has located the problem within herself and thus strives to challenge herself 'all the time'. When I reflected on the participants' words, it was evident to me that a further exploration was required to make explicit that the 'internal narratives' that I had identified did not arrive from within but, of course, from external areas of their lives. Their experiences were understood and created the 'internal narrative'. When this is happening to a child in their developmental period, we might think about those narratives as forming while the child and/or young person is 'wiring up', hence the internalisation into identity. When I considered some of the existing ways that children in care are represented, my focus around stigma was supported; children in care are represented in overly positive or overly negative ways by professionals and by the media, keeping stigmatisation alive. Identities develop through the sense making of a person's story which is not static but rather a co-creation between the person and those around them (Roberts and Dutton, 2009). In other words, it is relational and experiential.

Types of Stigma

I interpreted diverse types of stigma faced specifically by children in care in two ways; systemic (professional and social) and individual (self-stigma). Professional stigma can be found in professional practice. It can be found in the language used between professionals that can sometimes end up as recordings in files held about children that they go on to read as adults. This might show up in the form of jargon or opinions. It can also be found in views held by some working within the care system; they may share social attitudes towards aspects of the lives experienced by children in care and their families such as parental incarceration, abuse, neglect, exclusion, racism, classism, sexism or ideas about what children who are in care might deserve.

On a systemic level, the stigma narratives internalised were of the mechanics of being in care. This manifested, for example, through living in certain children's homes, through being in or from certain parts of a town and from being from families previously known to services and from being in prison. Some of these stigma narratives are expressed below.

Lost in the system.

(Jenny)

It (the children's home) was where all the bad boys went.

(James)

You're lucky to get fostered.

(Crystal)

You're looked after by the state.

(Matthew)

Teachers said I wouldn't amount to much like my mum.

(Matthew)

The experience of being in care then intersected with many other aspects of marginalisation such as race, class and poverty.

I was bullied for being mixed race.

(Jenny)

The only black kid and feeling 'not normal'.

(James)

I have never felt like I fit in in England particularly as it has not been very kind to me as a place.

(Sam)

On an individual level, this systemic view appeared to then be internalised in how the experiences were understood and were either then assimilated or rejected.

I wasn't good enough … I was deemed a high risk.

(Maisie)

> *My understanding was I wasn't good enough for foster care, so I went into a children's home.*
>
> (Maisie)

> *I was always like the naughty kid.*
>
> (Jenny)

> *I was maladjusted.*
>
> (James)

> *I felt hated.*
>
> (Crystal)

> *I felt flawed.*
>
> (Donna)

> *I felt I was naughty.*
>
> (Alisha)

> *It's like there was something wrong with me, that nobody wanted me.*
>
> (Shannon)

With this gathered wisdom, we are given an opportunity to think about the internal dialogue that might occur when the tension between how someone perceives themselves collides with systemic stigmatisation and self-perception.

> *I begged my social worker to not take me there because I already knew that the school had a reputation and it's where what we consider where all the bad boys went an' I didn't think I was a bad boy.*
>
> (James)

The wisdom shared conveyed systemic stigmatisation that was then internalised by the individual. The individual might not have described themself as stigmatised. However, the language used informed my interpretation of what I read: stigma was present in society and in professional practice, which subsequently formed a narrative that impacted on identity formation and the development of self-stigma. This is aligned with Andersen et al.'s (2022) view on stigma being experienced by groups, which causes individuals suffering.

This movement between systemic stigmatisation and how this impacts those using those systems warrants further exploration. It is not straightforward to theorise about 'stigma' as theories are contested, rejected and potentially deemed inadequate, including by those who have experienced it. Theory does, however, provide a medium for exploring the narratives shared. The complexity is intensified for the participants who experienced systemic stigma or professional stigma, which then became internalised.

The multi-layered complexity becomes harder to unweave when those who have experienced the stigma of care go on to work in professions such as social work or education, greeting the stigma from another dimension.

> *Now I'm a safeguarding social worker would you believe and I often think what on Earth am I doing, you know, doing this job given my background given my knowledge of how it affected my own children.*
>
> (Donna)

> *Now I've actually done social work and also research into modern slavery I'd say one of the things that really stood out is the labels that they put on you from your outcomes.*
>
> (Jenny)

> *I thought becoming a social worker would change how I viewed things but it has reinforced the oppression. Fighting as a child, fighting that oppression, fighting that discrimination to then have to do that as an adult and as a professional.*
>
> (Alisha)

Deep intersections of stigmatisation are nestled between being in care and school exclusion, and are intertwined with experiences of ethnicity, race and class. One participant talks about the experience of being from the gypsy traveller community.

> *I was treated very differently to the others. The other people that were there in most of the schools because of my background from where I came from because I was a traveller and because I was like I think it was, you know different and that just made me feel like I have to always be on edge like ready to ... I don't know.*
>
> (Shannon)

Powell (2008) writes that 'the persistence of stigma in relation to British nomadism runs so deep that the Commission for Racial Equality (2006) concluded that Gypsies and Irish Travellers are the most excluded groups in Britain today' (p. 88), echoed recently by Brassington (2022).

Some participants further highlighted the complex intersection of care and educational exclusion with being racialised as black or brown.

> *Ofsted says it's amazing. Outstanding. It was one of the best schools in the area that wasn't a private school and going into there, already you kind of feel like an outsider because of your race and also ... because I was kind of the only brown child in there.*
>
> (Jenny)

> *As a black boy (mixed race – increasing my sense of not being one or another) I didn't feel I belonged where I found myself; a children's home in a new town on the outskirts of London.*
>
> (James)

The intersection of care and school exclusion with class and racism was also raised, and demonstrates the multiplicity of the experience of marginalisation and stigmatisation.

> *I lived with my grandparents until I was 10 and it was quite a middle-class upbringing. I didn't realise I was different in any way and then my mum wanted to move out of there and she got a council house. That setting was really awful for mum. I had a lot of kind of racist attacks then because I'm mixed and I didn't realise I was any different before that, so that was really hard on me. I guess from that, that's when I kind of started to kind of run away and just be kind of crazy and not going to school and stuff like that.*
>
> (Sam)

This wisdom offers strong indications not only of how stigma exists in society and in professional discourse, but also of how it impacts an individual's identity during development and well into adulthood. There are layers of experience that are stigmatised and stigmatising, and they interweave to create a sense of disconnection and confusion about how a person makes sense of who they are and where they belong. Connecting stigma with trauma further adds to understanding how this impacts on belonging.

Let's Take A Moment …

You've just read pages of people's expressions of trauma and pain and hurt and sorrow and there is more to follow. It's time to pause, take a breath and notice what you're feeling. What is showing up for you in your body? Where can you feel it? In your chest, your heart, your shoulders? What words are coming forward in your mind? Notice what is happening to you and deepen your own self-awareness. Do you need to pause? Do you need to self-hug with your arms like we often shared with one another during Covid lockdowns? Remember, we can't be immersed in trauma without it impacting us in some way so self-awareness that supports us in responding to ourselves and our needs is how we can show up as our best selves for those we serve.

Trauma and Stigma

Trauma originates from the Greek word *traumata* meaning to wound or damage, however the entry of the word 'trauma' into the lexicon of understanding the impact of harm during the developmental period of childhood has only recently become more widely acknowledged. There is a greater understanding of how psychological trauma is the result of distress and a way of thinking about the impact of 'what happened to a person', rather than viewing what the distress presented as being 'what is wrong with this person'.

The lens of viewing the impact of experiences endured during the childhood developmental period highlighted 'trauma' as another theme. The literature on trauma provided fertile ground on which to develop a sensitivity to the wisdom provided by the participants that indicated their experiences of trauma; nonetheless, even if I had not had that sensitivity, some of the participants themselves used the word 'trauma' to describe their experiences.

> *My experience of care was pretty traumatic.*
>
> (Maisie)

> *My mother equally went through trauma, so we're a result of her trauma.*
>
> (Donna)

> *My childhood was disrupted and so my childhood, you know, I perhaps didn't develop as my friends did or people who didn't experience childhood trauma.*
>
> (Alisha)

Diagnoses and disorders were widely raised in the participants' experiences and although trauma does not mean that the inevitable outcome will be a mental health diagnosis, or that a mental health diagnosis will always be the outcome of trauma, the literature suggests that the two can be interchangeable. In other words, a diagnosis might well locate the problem in the individual without further investigation of past unhealed traumas. This can create a lifetime reliant on medication instead of access to trauma therapies. Poor mental health as a response to trauma did arise in participants' experiences and demonstrated a difference between those who used and had an understanding of a trauma lens, and those who used the diagnostic language of mental disorders lens.

> *Post Traumatic Stress Disorder.*
>
> (Jenny, Shaun, Maisie)

> *Social Anxiety Disorder.*
>
> (Matthew)

Attention Deficit Hyperactivity Disorder.

(Matthew)

Paranoid Schizophrenia.

(Shaun)

Split Personality Disorder.

(Shaun)

Memories

All the participants recalled memories of events that brought traumatic experiences to the fore. Some examples are highlighted below. For example, Maisie, recalls vivid memories of the inside of a 'secure unit' which she arrived at as a 13-year-old. As an adult she recalls sleeping in a bedroom rather than a cell as a reward. She is able to describe the inside of the cell and while she did not describe this as traumatic, this element of the interview was given amidst a catalogue of remembered 'homes' during her time in care as a young teenager.

> *When I first went in there, you like, walk down the corridor and then you go into the cells and those bedrooms upstairs. But you had to earn points to go and sleep in a bedroom and it was like a bare concrete cell and there was just a crash mat on the floor like no wooden furniture or nothing.*
>
> (Maisie)

Throughout the interview, Maisie used the word 'trauma' four times and the word 'traumatic' twice explicitly referencing her time in care as a 'traumatic experience'. In referencing trauma, she describes isolation, aloneness and having nothing. However, at this stage of her life, she reflects on the friends that care about her:

> *I've got like this life that I've created for myself that sometimes I feel like I don't deserve 'cause you get that impostor syndrome and stuff, don't you, but I've got real true friends that care about me. Knowing like where I am now compared to where I was. It's more of a journey, isn't it?*
>
> (Maisie)

Others, such as Jenny, did not use the word 'trauma', but described what are commonly recognised as traumatic events:

> *I'm also a survivor of modern day slavery and I would say that all the vulnerability factors stemmed back from when I was in care.*
>
> (Jenny)

Furthermore, the implicitly traumatic experience of the loss of his mother at a young age was recalled by Shaun:

> *My mother was the only person I did trust growing up. I didn't trust nobody else. Like I'd phone her from everywhere I went and like they were taking me to visit her every weekend because she was asking and when they talked to me she didn't know how to cope. I had to take care of my brother. I had to feed him and change him as I was only 12 and they've took me in care again and so my mother found it hard like. I mean she went and lived with my Nana and then my father's mom. My brother's father took my brother off my mother so that affected her in a big way. Then she had a lung transplant. Then she died. I was in prison, I was.*
>
> (Shaun)

It is widely understood that parental death in childhood during the years of development, understood to be during most of our time in utero to around 25 years old, is a traumatic event and bereaved children can be at an increased risk of developing mental health issues in adulthood (Azuike et al., 2022). Moreover, Shaun describes going into care 'as the worst time of my life' which happened prior to his mother's death. He also talks about having a diagnosis for Post Traumatic Stress Disorder (PTSD), Attention Deficit Hyperactivity Disorder (ADHD), Paranoid Schizophrenia and Split Personality Disorder and in so doing is very aware of his own poor mental health. Moving forward from his experiences, he attributes where he is today to the organisation supporting him and his new partner. My interpretation of his account of what happened to him was that he was in the early stages of making sense of his experiences, but was clearer about what helped him to achieve Post Traumatic Growth (PTG), namely in both personal and professional relationships.

Whether the participants shared diagnoses, events or the manifestations of dealing with distress, trauma provided the background soundtrack. In speaking of trauma, whether explicitly or implicitly, the participants made reference to abuse, exploitation, violence, isolation and neglect. Key characteristics that come through in the accounts of trauma are powerlessness and isolation. Traumatic events recollected refer to 'feeling scared' and 'lost' (James) and that 'care was extremely abusive' (Donna). 'Where are the relationships?' asks Matthew while speaking about being isolated in school. For Shaun, saying 'bad things happened ... really bad' was as much as he could share.

One participant spoke vividly of powerlessness, sexual and physical abuse and neglect with a great deal of detail:

> *Even the nurses behaving inappropriately trying to get me to go and see adult films and so on, you know it was really shocking and I was actually groomed there by somebody and so now I think if children are groomed*

> *like that, it would be considered statutory rape, yeah? It was horrible.*
>
> (Donna)

Other participants also went into detail about what had happened to them:

> *As a child it wasn't my responsibility to build relationships with adults that couldn't trust, because even by then I was being sexually abused. I've been physically abused. I've been neglected.*
>
> (Maisie)

> *Mum alcoholic, dad drug dealer and shot himself in front of me when I was young.*
>
> (Shannon)

In line with other scholars (e.g. Herman, 2001; Rothschild, 2010; Van Der Kolk, 2015) my reflection is that trauma is, among other things, about a loss of power, and a sense of powerlessness. There are numerous accounts of trauma recounted in the experiences of those who took part in the research, but trauma was expressly recognised and defined in these terms by only a few of the participants. By investigating the detail and experience of trauma such as the impact on these individuals as a child and into adulthood, we can extend our understanding of the impact of trauma and the long shadow that it casts.

Stigma and Power

Like trauma, power is a thread that runs explicitly and implicitly through the wisdom gifted by the participants, and this is also unsurprising. Unlike trauma, power is barely referenced but is identifiable in the detailed accounts, mostly where trauma is being described. Where children are concerned, the 'state', which intervenes in the family, the care system and the compulsory education system are settings and systems that do 'to' a child rather than 'with' a child, particularly when those two systems, care and education, collide, rendering a child powerless. Could this be the seat of the wound?

To further consider the issue of power, it can be thought of in three distinct areas:

- Coercive power – state intervention and abuses of that intervention, physically and sexually, control around family access.
- Professional power – demonstrated through practices that silence, isolate and restrain using legislation and policy, the power to move a child from their home.
- Economic power – demonstrated through poverty in childhood, poverty after care, austerity and access to education, access to help and support.

Using a trauma lens to view childhood experiences, such as abuse and neglect, locates power and the powerlessness experienced at the heart of the experience. However, power has traditionally been left out of the psychiatric discourse on emotional distress (Boyle, 2022). This can be observed in the more recently developed Power Threat Meaning Framework (PTMF), a collective and inclusive endeavour that has sought to develop an alternative lens to the diagnostic model of distress and mental illness (Johnstone, 2022). PTMF focuses on meaning making rather than biology and is premised on the idea that the meaning making is individual and not fixed. If I return your thoughts to Chapter 1 where I spoke of the experience of reading my contribution to the original text of my book *The Brightness of Stars*, the meaning making had shifted over time. We are not fixed in how we make sense of the world because we develop and grow dynamically in relationship to our environment and the relationships that we have around us. I would also add in relationship to the opportunities that we may be lucky enough to have presented to us. Additionally, the patterns of threat responses (rather than symptoms) are about what people 'do' rather than what they 'have' (a diagnosis) in relation to mental health diagnoses (Johnstone, 2022, p. 16).

Aspects of Power

In considering the powerlessness that those who took part in my research highlighted, different aspects of power arose. These are embodied, coercive, legal, economic, interpersonal, social/cultural and ideological (Boyle, 2022). For example, Maisie said:

> I already had all these professionals involved in these people talking about me deciding what they knew was best. I don't remember being included in any of their meetings.
>
> (Maisie)

Feeling that she was not included, not accepted and not involved not only speaks to the lack of control and agency she felt in her own life, but also potentially of what 'unbelonging' might feel like. Others knew best, and she felt there was no way of having her voice heard:

> You're not in secure accommodation, because although you can't leave, you know it's not prison, but actually it was. If it was looked at in this context, I wasn't able to leave. I wasn't able to go out when I wanted. I had my whole teenage years being restrained in a unit where if I left the grounds or if I went out on a company, I would get arrested.
>
> (Crystal)

Power comes through here in Crystal's descriptions in the form of being restrained (physical violence), and of being unable to leave the building when she wanted without being arrested, and the power then exercised by the police in an arrest. Here, power is intrinsically connected to feelings of safety and of having freedom.

In a different way of thinking about power, Sam talks about the experience of being a woman of mixed race living on a council estate.

> *You know, for me, social exclusion is not being made to feel a human being. It's like a mix of things so yeah, there's many kind of levels to it if you know what I mean and so I wasn't just mixed race. I was a female. I was living on a council estate, you know. So there was a lot of things against me.*
>
> (Sam)

These are all experiences that are visible and in bringing them together Sam highlights intersectional disadvantage and social exclusion, which will be explored further in Chapter 8. Stigmatisation serves to keep people in their place and those who experience stigma are rarely seen in power, although the Cabinet of the government which was formed in 2024 had people on the front benches who had experienced poverty, single parenting and being gay, for example. The stigma is the visibility of those experiences and stigma is a form of power exercised over others (Tyler, 2020). In other words, it is difficult to talk about stigma without also talking about power. Stigma makes power visible by penetrating the development of identity and the way that identity moves around their environment. Maybe we can move away from the idea of the 'person in power' and 'the powerless' which is a binary approach. But before we do that, understanding that stigma and power work together will help us develop more nuanced ways to escape from this relationship. Moreover, the connection between power and trauma needs attention. Trauma, power and stigma are interrelated.

Summary

Stigma, trauma and power are inextricably linked. These collective levers leave a deep impression on the individual and are connected to the way a person has made meaning of the events they have experienced, the relationships and opportunities available to them and the ability of the person to access those relationships and opportunities. The participants' accounts here also indicate how difficult it can be to break free from this toxic web, though not impossible, many of us are testament to that, but it is difficult all the same.

Stigma, trauma and power are interrelated, intersectional and multi-layered. Identifiably, there is professional stigma which is found in the language used in practice and in policy by professionals such as educators, social workers and the police. The language of legislation finds its way into professional parlance which is then internalised by children and young people. This question of 'language' is further explored in Chapter 5. Additionally, social stigma is present and this refers to the lived experience of being in care, of being excluded from school and of racism and how society, at any given time, provides narratives for these experiences. Finally, self stigma refers to the internal narrative developed through the exposure of professional and social stigma, which manifests in low self-worth, lack of confidence and patterns of behaviour that are recreated from childhood experiences.

Types of trauma (not an exhaustive list):

- Neglect
- Physical abuse
- Sexual abuse
- Polyvictimisation
- Community trauma
- Child trafficking
- System harm
- Homelessness
- State intervention

- Exclusion
- Poverty
- Living in care
- Racism
- Bereavement of a parent.

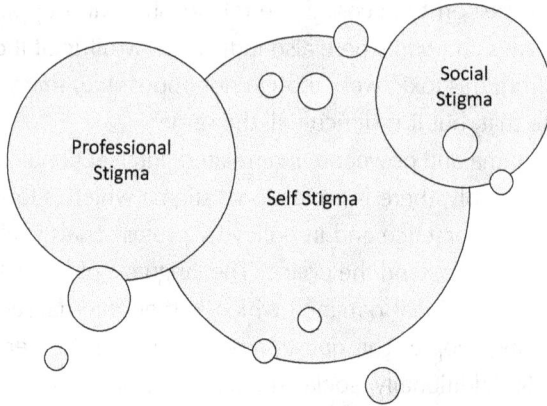

Figure 3.2   Stigma Types

Professional stigma refers to the language used by practitioners and also includes historical notions of 'care' and the 'deserving poor' alongside personal beliefs held by, for example, educators, social workers and the police. Social stigma refers to the stigmatisation within society around, for example, how the public perceive the reason why a child is living in care, how a children's home is viewed (there is usually a local outcry when planning permission is requested for a new children's home), school exclusion and racism. Self stigma is a term adopted in this book to describe how these experiences of professional and social stigma impact on identity, a sense of 'unbelonging', low self-worth, self-esteem and general internal narratives regarding the experiences of children's services and education. In Chapter 4 we delve into the impact of 'unbelonging'.

Key Chapter Takeaways

- Movement and stigma are connected and create a sense of unbelonging that is layered when that movement is instigated by legislation. Power and trauma often work collectively to further the experience of and internalisation of stigmatisation.
- Power can be considered as professional, coercive or economic.
- Trauma, power and stigma are connected, forming layers of unbelonging that are interwoven into settings, services and systems.

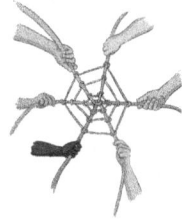

Reflection

In what ways has thinking about trauma, power and stigma helped your understanding about working with children and young people facing disadvantage, vulnerabilities and adversity? Is thinking about stigma helpful? What is your own experience of stigma? In what ways can /does your setting actively reduce stigmatisation?

References and Bibliography

Andersen, M. M., Varga, S., & Folker, A. P. (2022). On the definition of stigma. *Journal of Evaluation in Clinical Practice*, 28(5): 847–853.

Azuike, P., Anjoyeb, M., & King, L. (2022). Bereavement and children's mental health: recognising the effects of early parental loss. *Nursing Children and Young People*, 34(1): 26– 32.

Boyle, M. (2022). Power in the Power Threat Meaning Framework. *Journal of Constructivist Psychology*, 35(1): 27–40.

Brassington, L. (2022). Gypsies, Roma and travellers: the ethnic minorities most excluded. Retrieved on 22 November 2024 from https://www.hepi .ac.uk/wp-content/uploads/2022/07/Gypsies-Roma-and-Travellers.pdf

Commission for Racial Equality. (2006). https://www.gov.uk/government/ publications/commission-for-racial-equality-annual-report-and-accounts -2006-to-2007

Crenshaw, K. (1991). Mapping the margins: intersectionality, identity politics, and violence against women of color. *Stanford Law Review*, 43(6): 1241–1299.

Goffman, E. (1963). *Stigma: Notes on the Management of Spoiled Identity*. Englewood Cliffs, NJ: Prentice-Hall.

Herman, J. L. *(2001). Trauma and Recovery*. New York: Basic Books.

Johnstone, L. (2022). General patterns in the Power Threat Meaning Framework – principles and practice. *Journal of Constructivist Psychology*, 35(1): 16–26.

Link, B. G., & Phelan, J. C. (2001). 'Conceptualizing stigma. *Annual Review of Sociology*, 27(1): 363–385.

Manago, B., Davis, J. L., & Goar, C. (2022). The Stigma Discourse-Value Framework. *Comparative Sociology*, 21(3): 275–299.

Pescosolido, B. A., & Martin, J. K. (2015). The Stigma Complex. *Annual Review of Sociology*, 41(1): 87–116.

Powell, R. (2008). Understanding the stigmatization of gypsies: power and the dialectics of (dis)identification. *Housing, Theory, and Society*, 25(2): 87–109.

Roberts, L. M., & Dutton, J. E. (2009). *Exploring Positive Identities and Organisations: Building a Theoretical and Research Foundation*. Abingdon: Routledge.

Rothschild, B. (2010). *8 Keys to Safe Trauma Recovery: Take-charge Strategies to Empower Your Healing* (1st ed.). New York: W.W. Norton.

Tyler, I. (2020). *Stigma: The Machinery of Inequality* (1st ed.). London: Bloomsbury Publishing.

Van der Kolk, B. (2015). *The Body Keeps the Score: Brain, Mind, and Body in the Healing of Trauma*. New York: Penguin.

4

The Impact of Unbelonging

Introduction

The marginalisation and disadvantaging of children and young people is not a new issue. Certain children and their families have endured such treatment historically across centuries. This probably explains why societal and sector attitudes, current legislation and policy and education and children's social care sectors are intertwined even though both sectors are formed as though they are entirely separate. In this chapter, the impact of this legacy is explored.

We don't have to do much searching to find out just how well documented it is that those leaving care have poorer outcomes in health and education than their peers. The LACGro Project (2021) and many other researchers of children in care and care leavers document these differential outcomes; potentially this is a leftover from the earlier work which sought to provide an understanding of the importance of prioritising children who were in care. My resistance to begin this chapter in the same way as earlier works is because there are many places to read those introductions that tell a single story. However, it is my intention to make space for other experiences. I am hoping that you will be able to explore other experiences further in your own practice by considering the data and lived experiences of those you work with. However, in doing so, it must be borne in mind that such data captures a moment in time and until the body of work in which researchers ask

DOI: 10.4324/9781003426592-6

adults with those experiences to reflect back, the narrative of poor outcomes vs freak success will never change.

The outcomes of those who were in care as children can be better understood as being on a life course spectrum dependent on age, experiences, relational opportunities, access to education and personality. The Department for Education (DfE) (2022) collected information about those in care at 17, 18, 19, 20 and 21 years old to identify the number of care leavers 'in touch' with their local authority. This information comprises whether they are in education, employment or training and the reasons for this not being the case, and whether the accommodation they are living in (they are still looked after between 16 and 18) is regarded as suitable. Also, data collected on those over 21 years old who are therefore outside the data is usually collected when accessing a particular service, for example, mental health services, criminal justice settings and housing departments.

Collecting administrative data in this way presents a bleak picture of life for an adult who has experience of the care system. It doesn't reflect the complexities of how we develop across the life course. This is not to belittle the seriousness of the specific vulnerabilities of those who have been in care, but rather to suggest that the outcomes of being in care should not be presented as a description that contributes towards shame and stigmatisation. For example, according to such data, 31 per cent of women and 24 per cent of men within the prison population had spent time in the care system as a child (Ministry of Justice, 2018). More recently, the Office for National Statistics (2022) showed that more than half (52 per cent) of looked-after children born in the academic year ending 1994 who attended school in England had a criminal conviction by the age of 24 compared with 13 per cent of children who had not been in care. This also means that 48 per cent of looked-after children did *not* have a criminal record by the age of 24. However, that is notwithstanding the concern that should be at the forefront of policy makers' minds regarding such an eye-wateringly high number of looked-after children gaining a criminal conviction. That said, it is crucial that policy accounts for what has been termed an 'invisible minority' (Care Leavers Association, 2019). Nor can we ignore the positive stories as this creates another 'invisible minority'. As professionals working with children and young people, it is our responsibility to report the many, very different stories to be told about the care experience.

In this chapter, although I will still make clear the challenges faced by those who are care experienced, I invite you to consider that there are many other outcomes which can be arrived at different points of a person's life that are never asked about. What is success? Having an intimate relationship that is healthy? Or is achieving education at a later stage in life still an important life outcome? Maybe it is having friends and a broad network.

I would also argue that it is possible that information about success or gathering wisdom such as this from adults with lived experience of care, particularly adults who were excluded from school, is not sought because it is simply not desired. I suggest this because there are statutory obligations to understand children that simply do not exist for adults. Knowledge acquired from adults reflecting on difficult childhood experiences has not previously been deemed useful knowledge that has the potential to influence policy and practice. This is changing, albeit slowly.

Language

Language shapes how we make sense of the world, our experiences and the experiences of others and this is particularly the case for those living with the experience of being in care or having been in care. The term 'looked after child' is a legal term under the Children Act 1989 and applies to children under 18 years of age who are subject to a placement, care order or are supplied with accommodation by the local authority children's services for more than 24 hours. 'Care leaver' is also a legal term which refers to those over the age of 16 who meet certain criteria which ensures they will receive support up to the age of 25 in certain circumstances. However, the Care Leavers Association is clear in acknowledging that the experience of being in care extends across the life course and they have expanded the definition to refer to any adult who spent time in care as a child. Some people prefer the term 'care experienced', which is the term used in Scotland in *The Promise* (Scottish Government, 2020) and was chosen in collaboration and consultation with those with care experience. This is a great example of what can be achieved when we practise working using a co-production model.

This interchangeable use of terminology serves as a useful reminder to us all that legal or institutional language can be simultaneously othering and inclusive, particularly when not chosen by the person who has experienced marginalisation. The use of the term 'education' in this book is used to mean compulsory education. However, what has counted as compulsory education has changed over the last few decades. For example, the age that one could leave compulsory education was raised from 14 years old to 16 years old in 1972. In England, the age was raised again to 17 years old in 2013 and to 18 years old in 2015. In Scotland, Wales and Northern Ireland, the compulsory leaving age is 16 years old. The latest guidance on school exclusions differentiates between a suspension, which was previously known as a fixed-term exclusion and can last for a maximum of 45 days in an academic year, and an exclusion, which refers to permanent removal from the education setting (DfE, 2022). We must also remember that there are other educational facilities apart from schools. Some residential units also offer educational facilities as do other settings such as secure units, medical provisions or young offenders' provisions. Exclusions may well have taken place in some of these other settings as well as in what we understand to be traditional (mainstream) schools. Perhaps you can think of further facilities that would fit this purpose too.

The complexity of the cultural, legislative and historical shifts over time which frame the experiences of school exclusion means that being a child in care and being in education will have impacted each individual differently. We write our own stories when it comes to making sense of our own experiences.

Language and Labelling

Language can be verbal or non-verbal, spoken and/or written. In Chapter 5, I argue that it can be used as a tool of power and can harm or heal (Cherry, 2023). Children in care often share with us that they were subjected to language that can harm within education settings (Jones et al., 2020). An example of this is the term 'looked-after child' which we often see in policy and practice documents as the acronym LAC. It makes so many children and young people ask the question, 'Does this mean I am lacking in something'? (NSPCC, 2023). The Adolescent and Children's Trust (TACT) co-created and developed with care-experienced children and young people from across England a document called 'Language That Cares' (TACT, 2019). They included commentary on a great deal of terminology that was disliked by the contributors, such as 'not in employment, education or training' (NEET), 'LAC', 'placement' and 'respite', which was highlighted with alternatives given.

> Respite: a short period of rest or relief from something difficult or unpleasant.

Expanding on this work, the Children's Safeguarding Board in Staffordshire co-produced a dictionary (The Voice Project, 2021), whilst being very aware of the power of language and the role it has in shaping identity. I am pleased to share that cultivating belonging to minimise the impact of stigmatisation is now very much a consideration when many services and local authorities think about their work with children and young people in their care. There is a body of research on language and how it can stigmatise those with poor mental health through labelling and terminology that serves to 'other' the person using the service when utilised by the person delivering the service (Ashford et al., 2019). However, for those of you who enjoy research, there is little on the language used within children's services about children in care and their families, and how terminology perpetuates stigma. I'm hopeful that one of you will ask this research question and add to the discussion.

Children in Care

Out of the nearly 12 million children living in England, just over 400,000 (3 per cent) are in the social care system at any one time. In 2024, nearly 84,000 of these children were in care and this number keeps rising (DfE, 2024). Seventy-three per cent were described as being of white ethnicity, 10 per cent mixed, with 7 per cent described as black African, Caribbean or black British. Finally, 5 per cent were Asian or Asian British. 'Other' was at 4 per cent with those where ethnicity was not recorded being 1 per cent (DfE, 2022). These data are not broken down by age. Currently, males account for 66 per cent of all looked-after children and females account for 44 per cent with no category included that understands or considers gender identification. Not only are the placement and service needs of LGBTQIA+ youth not always adequately addressed (Lopez Lopez et al., 2021), to make matters even worse, this data is not collected. How can we structure inclusive data which meets the needs of young people without critical information?

The category of needs recorded by the DfE states that 66 per cent came into care due to *abuse or neglect*, 2 per cent due to *the child's disability*, 3 per cent due to *parental illness or disability*, 7 per cent due to *the family being in acute stress*, 13 per cent due to *family dysfunction*, 1 per cent due to *socially unacceptable behaviour* and 7 per cent due to *absent parenting* (DfE, 2022). As already shown in earlier chapters, children in care and those leaving care have long been identified as vulnerable, experiencing poorer educational and longer-term outcomes than children and young people who are not care experienced. In an interesting study by Barnardo's (2021), 25 per cent of the homeless population were estimated to have been in care and 39 per cent of care leavers aged 19–21 years were not in education, employment or training, highlighting that since 2010, the number of children in care in England has continued to rise. As stated earlier, there were nearly 84,000 children in care which is a rise from 64,460 in 2010 (DfE, 2022). During the same period, the number of unaccompanied asylum-seeker children rose from 3,490 to 7,290. I am using the period of 2010 to the present date to reflect on very specific events that could be relevant to this rise. However, in doing so, I very much acknowledge that there is complexity and I have no intention of being deductive, merely explorative with intention.

If we cast our minds back to the ideology of austerity which was mentioned in the introduction, we saw harsh welfare reform. Preventative and protective services were hit hard and there was a sharp rise in what became known as 'poverty porn' exploiting division and stigma (Cooper and Whyte, 2017; Tyler, 2020). The rise in youth knife crime during this time, peaking in 2017/2018, was argued by some as being interconnected with the austerity agenda (Thapar, 2021; Younge, 2017). Virdee and McGeever (2018) argue that Brexit brought more divisive politics and was underpinned by the slogan of 'taking back control' which invariably brought race, racism and xenophobia to the fore, and led to racist hate crimes.

Brexit was followed by the global pandemic and various lockdowns enforced by the government in a bid to quell infection. The number of children needing foster care rose by 44 per cent during the pandemic but at the same time the number of those looking to become foster parents fell by half (Barnardo's, 2020). High-profile child protection situations also intensify concerns in society and therefore put pressure on the system. This can lead to a risk averse climate of practice in which social workers and all those involved in safeguarding children and young people are situated. In the last 12 years alone, the deaths of children in the hands of abusers, such as 4-year-old Daniel Pelka (2012), 4-year-old Hamzah Khan (2013), 6-year-old Arthur Labinjo-Hughes (2020) and 16-month-old Star Hobson (2021) made the headlines and created individual serious case reviews that provided enough evidence to change the culture of child protection.

In addition, the rising number of children needing to come into care could be accounted for by the impact of environmental harm on the Global South, which has increased the number of those fleeing affected countries and ongoing wars; this potentially explains the rise in unaccompanied minors entering care, as highlighted above. Another potential explanation for the rise in the number of children coming into care could be found in the expansion of those living in poverty, as a result of the 'cost of living crisis'. A longitudinal study between 2015 and 2020 found evidence that rising child poverty rates contributed to an increase in the number of children entering care, noting that children who are exposed to poverty are more likely to experience more adversity, which is associated with poor health and social outcomes across the life course (Bennett et al., 2022). Since then, the 'cost of living crisis', as termed by politicians, has taken hold more deeply. Drawing attention to the worsening context highlights a spectrum of events that has impacted children, young people and their families in various ways. We must understand the socio-political impact on children in care of the state, and that the impact varies depending on the period of time and the focus that a particular government may or may not have on prevention and the protection and welfare of children. The very particular context that we find ourselves in has broad consequences for children and young people who rely on relationships, communities and settings for their protective factors.

The chances of children in care enjoying the same social and economic advantages in adulthood as other children are deeply unequal (The LACGro Project, 2021). The outcomes provide a bleak backdrop against which those in care, those leaving care and those who were children in care make sense of their lives. There has been some debate regarding whether the reasons for coming into care cause poor outcomes (Sebba et al., 2015) or whether care itself is the cause. Neuroscientists argue that we experience the world dynamically and that we develop over time with the relational experiences available to us (Eagleman, 2021), so it could be argued that there is no point in isolating a cause. The reasons for coming into care, care itself, the professional practices that envelop 'care' alongside how education and the community respond to those experiences and then how all those aspects interact with the individual and with their personality highlight the complexity of care and the care system. Therefore, administrative data, which currently only provide a one-dimensional view, is an important part of understanding the experience of care.

School Exclusion

As an adult who was permanently excluded from school, I am interested in what happens to children who are excluded. Exclusion, it seems to me, can act as an ending. The 'problem' is removed as far as some of those in the school are concerned, but it is the beginning for the child and their carers; the beginning of what? That is the question. although children and young people experience being removed from their school community, as adults they are unlikely to ever be asked for any research input. What happened? Where did you go? How did you feel? How did you overcome the impact? These are all questions that deserve to be asked.

Exclusion and Children in Care

Many of us would agree that the education of children in care is an area of concern but it has not always been viewed in that way. Researchers including Sonia Jackson have worked tirelessly on the education of children in care. Jackson shared many of her early findings in her seminal text *The Education of Children in Care* (1987). She expressed concerns about the lack of statistical data on the educational outcomes of children in care together with anecdotal experiences of poorer educational attainment and significant overrepresentation in all types of exclusions. There are many complex and intersecting factors that make understanding educational outcomes challenging including length of time in placement, number of placements, additional learning needs, ethnicity, gender, location of placement(s), reason for entry into care, to name a few. I can't unpack these in this book. However, a positive step in the right direction is that there is now statutory guidance from different departments to help agencies within local authorities to abide by the law in order to safeguard and promote the welfare as well as the educational achievement of those termed looked-after children and young people. This urges exclusion of children in care to be avoided.

School exclusion (legal permanent removal), 'off-rolling' (illegal permanent removal) and the use of 'isolation booths' (legal temporary removal) persist as hot, divisive issues (Condliffe, 2023; Martin-Denham, 2020). However, children in care are still five times more likely to receive a fixed-period exclusion than their non-looked-after peers (DfE, 2020). Additionally, international comparisons show that children in care remain significantly overrepresented in suspensions (what were previously known as fixed-term exclusions) (Demie, 2021). Furthermore, when asked about exclusion, 2,000 adopters of those now known as 'previously looked after children' indicated that these children were 20 times more likely to be excluded than their peers (Adoption UK, 2017). How can this still be the case?

We must, however, always be cautious with data collected by the DfE regarding the exclusion of children in care as these are likely to be inaccurate with hidden exclusions such as 'managed moves', the use of isolation booths and unrecorded exclusion from the mainstream classroom or mainstream activities being used instead (Power and Taylor, 2020). In addition, the impact of Covid has heightened risk of exclusion as raised by the Excluded Lives Project (Daniels et al., 2020), an expansive project exploring the causes and consequences of school exclusion and the experiences of young people affected by it. Poor educational experiences potentially have life course implications, with care-experienced adults being more likely to experience homelessness, high unemployment and be involved with the criminal justice system (O'Higgins et al., 2017).

Education can be very powerful for the right reasons, with 70.1 per cent of care-experienced graduates working in a professional role or studying on a professional or postgraduate course compared with 72.3 per cent of other graduates six months after graduation (Harrison et al., 2022). This shows that education can alter the trajectories of those adults who were in care as children. Education levels the playing field. Where education is not readily accessible, whether through exclusion, constant home moves or unmet additional learning needs, children in care become more vulnerable to social exclusion and unemployment (Parker, 2017). In many cases, if we can understand the particular needs of children in care, we can ensure we get their educational experience right. This may mean we need to shift our perspective societally to account for the fact that strictly prescribed chronological milestones can be challenging for those children. This is particularly relevant when we consider that 30.2 per cent of children who have been continuously in care for 12 months or more have a special education need or disability (SEND) compared to 12.4 per cent of all other pupils, and social, emotional and mental health (SEMH) is the most common SEND at 51.2 per cent, in addition to children in care being 2.5 times more likely to access free school meals than other pupils (DfE, 2022).

Let's Take A Moment …

Grounding techniques take many forms and you've spent a lot of time in the cognitive part of your being. Academia is like that. It holds you in your brain rather than your body. It is a very cognitive space and I've just shared a lot of research and data and you're hoping to retain much of it, I imagine. A really good way to process what you're reading is to periodically use a completely different part of your being. So please don't be

surprised that I am now adding, mid chapter, a recipe for you. I know! If you don't like my favourite banana bread recipe, then choose something to prepare that you love. While you bake, or if that fills you with horror, then make something to eat that you do like, and eat slowly and mindfully. Of course, if you prefer to do this a little later, you can return to this page at any point that you feel you need to.

Banana Bread

Makes a 900g loaf and takes 10 minutes to prepare and about an hour to cook.

100g softened butter

125g castor sugar

2 large eggs

150g made up of sultanas, apricots, pecans or walnuts (and I like to add chocolate drops too)

Grated lemon zest

3 ripe large bananas

200g self-raising flour

Preheat the oven to 170 degrees. Line the base of your loaf tin. In a mixer (or by hand if you prefer), cream the butter and the sugar. When all blended, slowly add in the eggs. Then add your fruit and nuts. Add mashed bananas to the mix. Once combined, add the flour, carefully folding in to the mixture. Scrape the mixture into the loaf tin and bake. Insert a knife into the middle which should come out clean when the loaf is cooked. Depending on your oven, this will take somewhere between 50 and 60 minutes so don't wander off at this point. Once cooked, allow it to cool for at least 15 minutes, slice, add butter and enjoy with a cup of your favourite hot drink.

Now you will have processed your reading and you can now return to this book.

Trauma

People often wonder why children enter care. Abuse, which combines physical, sexual and emotional abuse into one category, accounts for the category given as the reason for being in care for the majority of children. Neglect is grouped statistically in this figure too and is defined in *Keeping Children Safe in Education* as 'the persistent failure to meet a child's basic physical, emotional and/or psychological needs, likely to result in the serious impairment of the child's health or development' (DfE, 2022, p. 108). Abuse and neglect could be considered as developmental trauma which refers to early ongoing and repetitive abusive or neglectful childhood experiences perpetrated by those who were meant to protect them during the developmental years, especially in the early years of life. This exposure can cause developmental harm (Perry, 2006; Van Der Kolk, 2015; Treisman, 2017; Golding, 2020).

When working with care-experienced children and adults, applying a trauma lens offers an opportunity to contextualise difficulty in forming relationships, difficulty in managing emotions and finding emotions overwhelming and detecting safety and finding chronological expectations unrealistic. Using a trauma lens refers to being sensitive to the impact of trauma on ourselves and on others that we are supporting.

This can provide another way of looking at social, emotional and mental health needs in educational contexts. Interestingly neurodivergent conditions and trauma tend to present in similar ways (Cox et al., 2018). Consequently, education settings that are more punitive in their approach to behaviour can be experienced as traumatic (Morgan and Costello, 2022). Whether children are care experienced or not, such approaches can feel overwhelming and unsafe without the relational support required. However, each of us experiences the world, including the relationships and connections we make, differently. Our early experiences impact us through the meaning we make of those experiences (Kishimi and Koga, 2019). Even the shape of the brain can change in response to our relational experiences – neuroscientists refer to this as plasticity. This is essentially the brain's capacity to reorganise the neuronal pathways that form our internal architecture in response to experiences and relationships (Eagleman, 2021). This not only helps us to understand that recovery from trauma is possible, it also helps us to understand why some people manage to live life without the poor outcomes associated with trauma in childhood (Voss et al., 2017).

However, focusing on the impact of trauma and adversity in childhood without also understanding the evidence and mechanisms at play when trying to comprehend that recovery is achievable is reductive, unhelpful and hindering. It means that some of the poor outcomes that may occur can be taken as certainties by some and are therefore taken as being the case for *all* care-experienced children and young people but this couldn't be further from the truth. The participants in my research demonstrate this beautifully as they were able to express that recovery takes time. Some of the participants referred to finding a community to belong to, having a family and being in nature as being the keys to overcoming trauma. This isn't to say that previous studies which documented challenges are wrong but reminds us that we must represent all outcomes including the positive ones (Schore, 2001; Porges, 2011; Siegel, 2010; Gerhardt, 2015). The participants in my research provide stories of hope which is an ingredient that we can all use in our work to create the kind of change that most of us are motivated to see.

I can probably speak for everyone reading this book that we would prefer to prevent and, indeed, eradicate trauma completely, this is highly unlikely. The next best thing? To accept we cannot be protected from everything and that, in fact, overcoming adversity brings unique and special gifts to the world. When we think about who we listen to, who inspires us, it will be somebody who has a story of recovery. If we accept that we appear unable to prevent war, neglect, community trauma, loss, poverty and unsafe housing, for example, our response can be

focused on building strong relational networks and robust communities for people so they can recover from adversity. Let's weave those webs of belonging!

If we focus on making meaning, understanding that what happens to us matters to us, this may help explain particularly difficult aspects of life experience when reflecting back as an adult. Using a trauma lens can provide the tools people need to work their way through a multitude of issues helping them understand the impact that they may experience regarding what happened to them.

Belonging

Attachment relationships and our motivational human needs are well documented. Most of childhood is usually spent within the home and available extended community initially and subsequently within educational settings and the larger community. What happens during developing years impacts humans and can provide the anchor on which children develop and grow (Shonkoff and Garner, 2012) and from which a sense of belonging is cultivated (Corrales et al., 2016). When home and school become fractured, what creates a sense of belonging? If we take the view that belonging is a fundamental human need, as Baumeister and Leary (1995) do, then this need must be met somewhere, and if it is not being met at home or within schooling then does its absence, as these authors go on to argue, have consequences and what are these consequences likely to be?

Table 4.1 Attachment Theory

Attachment Theory	Attachment theory, developed by John Bowlby and Mary Ainsworth, explores the significance of early relationships and bonds formed between caregivers and children. Within the care system, this theory underscores the importance of stable, nurturing relationships for children's emotional and psychological development.

Underpinning Theoretical Frameworks for Thinking about Belonging

For some of us, it may have been a little while since we were familiarised with attachment theory and for others, perhaps this may be the first time you have heard about it. So, here is a short summary of some of the most important elements. Back in the 1940s, Bowlby's work on attachment highlighted how important early childhood relationships are, which is now a well-accepted practice that I am sure almost every human would accept. His Attachment Theory, formed in 1969, explained this further. Mary Ainsworth created the Strange Situation study in 1970 to assess early relationships. She introduced the concept of attachment styles: secure, insecure avoidant and insecure ambivalent. Later, a fourth style, disorganised attachment, was added (Main and Solomon, 1986). Bowlby's theory emphasises that safety and connection form a critical foundation for children to base future relationships on. Infants with a secure attachment style are seen, safe, soothed and secure in the words of Siegel and Bryson (2020). However, it is possible for an infant to develop an insecure style if caregivers are unable to be consistent or neglect the needs of the infant. Disorganised attachment occurs when infants experience conflicting behaviours as a result of exposure to violence or frightening caregivers (Reisz et al., 2018). Critics argue the theory is too rigid and Western-centric (Smith et al., 2017). In their view, the Strange Situations method does not account for different ways of being a family and different caregiving systems, and Attachment Theory is potentially too inflexible (Röttger-Rössler, 2014). Focusing on attachment styles can prevent us from appreciating that attachment styles are fluid and can change over time (Webber, 2017). In response, the Dynamic Maturation Model is more flexible and thinks about attachment in terms of self-protective strategies that are connected to how the child interprets the environment and circumstances in which they find themselves (Crittenden, 2006). This model is much more strength-based and provides hope that it is still possible to build relationships and recover from traumatic experiences (Wilkerson,

Table 4.2 Hierarchy of Needs

Hierarchy of Needs	Maslow's model hierarchically locates the importance of belonging and has maintained its position of importance consistently across numerous disciplines including psychology, education and social work as a visual illustration of our human physical, psychological and emotional needs.

2010). Belonging and attachment are closely interrelated, starting with the dance of connection between a baby and their primary caregivers which establishes attachments that develop belonging, and having a sense of belonging creates attachments. A dance indeed. It might well be possible to argue that the presence of secure attachments can cultivate a sense of belonging (Chimange and Bond, 2020).

Another theoretical giant is Maslow, and his conceptualisation of the Hierarchy of Needs (Maslow, 1943).

This theory of human motivation appears to suggest that meeting these needs is a process and that without our physical needs being met, our ability to develop a sense of belonging is hampered. The pyramid suggests a progressive step-by-step approach to reaching 'actualisation' which starts with our physiological needs, then moves on to safety and security, then love and belonging, self-esteem and, finally, self-actualisation. The section on love and belonging was initially a section on love, but Maslow later expanded this area to include belonging to encompass friendship and giving and receiving affection (Rojas et al., 2023). The iconic pyramid strongly implies that the starting point is the lowest layer of needs and each layer of needs in Maslow's Hierarchy of Needs must be met in order to move to the next layer, which was described by Rojas et al. (2023) as sequential satisfaction. Furthermore, Rojas et al. go on to argue that the sequential structure of the model has led to a focus on basic human needs at the expense of our need for love and belonging and esteem.

There has been much criticism of Maslow's Hierarchy of Needs, not least that it was a study limited to highly educated white males (Mittelman, 1991) undertaken from an ethnocentric position (Bouzenita and Boulanouar, 2016). Therefore, within this structure, there is a focus on individualistic societies, on self-actualisation and self-fulfilment, as opposed to community and belonging (Hofstede, 1984). Further criticism of the model points to the omission of spirituality as a component and claims the commodification and overuse of the model divorces it from its meaning and sense of interdependence (Bouzenita and Boulanouar, 2016). Despite all these criticisms, these two theoretical routes to understanding belonging, Attachment Theory and Maslow's Hierarchy of Needs, both point to theoretical links to the human need to belong and it can be argued that it is as a result of Bowlby and Maslow's work that the idea of belonging has been firmly established in our work. Bronfenbrenner (1979) further develops how we think about belonging in the context of the world we live in and, for me, his model cements belonging as key, breaking down our ecosystem into spaces of influence.

Belonging is intrinsically linked to relationships, and a shift in emphasis from thinking in a linear way about the importance of meeting our basic needs before anything else may well need to involve a shift in focus to belonging as this has a considerable impact on people's sense of wellbeing (Rojas et al., 2023). It has been argued that a sense of belonging is dynamic, cultural and relational with an emotional complexity that can shift and change (Riley, 2022). Belonging is multi-dimensional and is conceived as thinking about belonging as something built up over time through everyday practices, as well as having membership or citizenship in a place (Antonsich, 2010).

Within psychology, belonging is defined as a yearning for connection rather than as an emotion and a need for positive regard (Rogers,

Table 4.3 Ecosystems Theory

Ecosystems Theory	Bronfenbrenner's Ecosystems Theory theorises that child development is impacted by a complex system of relationships and environmental influences which, when understood as working together, can cultivate belonging.

Table 4.4 Colonisation

Colonisation	Belonging, cultural identity and interconnectedness are fundamental ways of being for indigenous peoples. It is accepted that all life forms are connected; academic explorations with their theories and concepts are not necessary. Colonisation sought to destroy this inherent wisdom through the dispossession of land and denial of rights, policies of removal and dislocation, removal of language and names. Despite this, indigenous peoples maintain strong connections to their traditional lands, cultures and communities, preserving their unique sense of belonging. Many of the studies of the past and present require decolonising as the focus is often is white experiences. These critiques have been explored above but they also apply to the studies discussed below.

1951). Furthering that idea, developing a sense of belonging is measured by the extent to which a person feels accepted, respected and supported (Goodenow and Grady, 1993). Maslow's Hierarchy of Needs argues that physiological and safety needs have to be satisfied before love and a sense of belonging can emerge (Maslow, 1968, 1971) while Bronfenbrenner' Ecosystems Theory invites us to think about layers of belonging presented in concentric rings with the child in the centre (Bronfenbrenner, 1979).

Contemporary Comprehensions of Belonging

Some have argued (e.g. Sprince, 2015) that having a sense of belonging brings a coherent sense of self, with emotional intelligence, the capacity for self reflection and reflection on others, together with a capacity to collaborate. Belonging may be interpreted in different ways in the literature, and as Wright (2015) argues, its importance comes not necessarily from a stable meaning, but rather from the textured diversity of ways of feeling, doing, practising and living that are associated with it. The belonging lens offers a powerful way of viewing individuals which acknowledges human beings as social creatures, and that consequently they need to bond and form connections with others (Allen, 2021).

In addition to the fundamental theories on how we understand belonging as summarised above, the literature on belonging is extensive, covering a multitude of ways of thinking about belonging and of examining this very human experience. There are several popular books that simply refer to belonging (O'Donohue, 1998; Corless, 2021; hooks, 2009; Fuller, 2019). As someone who works extensively in developing trauma-informed settings, services and systems, I have come to understand that belonging is an antidote to trauma. In developing trauma-informed ways of working through practices that support those impacted by trauma to overcome those experiences, belonging can sit at the heart of our work, as an antidote to trauma. Trauma awareness helps us understand that trauma impacts us, while belonging offers the opportunity to create relationships which can heal.

Let's Take A Moment …

It is in the work of decolonisation that I think I have learnt the most. So entrenched are we in our own way of viewing the world that it can be challenging to imagine that all that we think we know is part of the problem itself. But, of course, our internal architecture is shaped and formed by the experiences that we have in the context of the relationships available to us. There are many ways to be human. Really embracing this helps us to have a cultural humility; I cannot know what I have not lived, the sixth trauma informed principle as laid out on page 82.

Developing a Trauma-informed Culture

It took decades of research on trauma and war veterans to understand that interpersonal violence, maltreatment and deprivation can impact children and young people in much the same way as war veterans experience PTSD (Van der Kolk, 2015). Amidst research on the impact of trauma in childhood came the breakthrough Adverse Childhood Experiences (ACEs) study, an epidemiological study of over 17,000 predominately middle-class, white adults, which identified that nearly two-thirds of adults had experienced trauma in their childhood (Felitti et al., 1998). The field of neuroscience went on to reveal that trauma affects brain development, is pervasive and can affect all areas of a person's life (Anda et al., 2006).

This interweaving of different disciplinary approaches to research on trauma, the ACEs study and the findings of neuroscience have led to the development of a more holistic understanding of how physical, social, emotional, cognitive and relational trauma and deprivation affect children and young people across their lifespan (Fellitti et al., 1998; Anda et al., 2006; Van Der Kolk, 2015).

Neuroscience points to changes in the neural development of children and young people who have been exposed to early life stress (ELS) which impact learning abilities related to IQ, attention, working memory, verbal ability and comprehension, but relational abilities are also impacted by challenges in emotion recognition, impulsivity and suppression of inappropriate actions (Hart and Rubia, 2012; Teicher et al., 2016). Trauma-informed programmes in education focus on the neurobiology of trauma to help teachers better understand why students have challenges in learning and why their responses to adverse situations in the classroom may appear, at times, impulsive, disruptive or inappropriate. Replacing school sanctions with emotion coaching techniques and restorative justice approaches are just a two of the methods used in trauma-informed practices to de-escalate conflict, avoid the re-traumatisation of children and young people and improve communication to build an emotionally safe and positive school climate.

Trauma-informed programmes raise awareness of the role of attachment disruption and reparation on student-teacher relationships and the need to build compassionate, nurturing relationships to repair trust in a climate of acceptance, belonging and care.

Trauma-informed frameworks, therefore, embed six core principles that respect, value, recognise and nurture transformative relationships with young people without re-traumatising them (SAMHSA, 2014). They emphasise:

1. Safety
2. Trustworthiness and transparency
3. Peer support
4. Collaboration and mutuality
5. Empowerment – voice and choice
6. Cultural, historical and gender issues.

For a school programme to be effective, each principle must be embedded in the organisation's culture as a whole-school approach

(Harris and Fallot, 2001) and must place the four Rs at the core of these principles (SAMHSA, 2014, p. 9):

1. **Realises** the widespread impact of trauma and understands potential paths for recovery
2. **Recognises** the signs and symptoms of trauma in children, families, staff and others involved with the system
3. **Responds** by fully integrating knowledge about trauma into policies, procedures and practices
4. **Resists** re-traumatisation.

Programmes must also align with the needs of the specific community and integrate cultural humility, inclusiveness and responsiveness by acknowledging 'historical and cultural trauma, oppression, social injustice, intersections of identity, & intergenerational trauma' (Treisman, 2021; NCTSN, 2021). Particular attention is paid to language which takes a counselling approach in an effort to avoid labels, offences, misintentions and conflict that re-traumatises.

This process of transforming a school environment so that it is truly trauma-informed takes training, time and commitment as it is not a linear process but it benefits all children and young people, regardless of their level of vulnerability. It also benefits teachers and schools, as having appropriate tools for more effective classroom management reduces stress levels and burnout (Berger and Martin, 2021). Developing a more compassionate school climate benefits everyone, including the adults as they too may have their own personal experience with trauma. A compassionate environment that replaces exclusions and sanctions with restorative practices improves the competency of the school to deliver stronger educational outcomes (Cherry, 2023).

The process of transitioning to a trauma-informed approach has often been likened to the flow of a river, it may not always be linear but it will embrace and smooth out the daily bumps that are encountered along the way (Treisman, 2021).

Staying with the focus on education settings, embedding trauma-informed and responsive practices begins by training schools, teachers, administrators and staff at a whole-school level. It can start with workshops on the neurobiology of attachment and trauma and identifying signs and behaviours that potentially reflect a history of trauma in student backgrounds, making key stakeholders 'trauma sensitive'. This includes, first, understanding the 'acting out cycle' and differentiating between fight, flight and freeze responses when students perceive a threat to their safety (Thomas et al., 2019). Secondly, it requires a multi-level collaborative effort to become 'trauma aware' by aligning trauma-informed principles with tangible actions that can affect change in the process of co-production with school administrators, teachers, staff and trainers (Cherry, 2023). Third, applying new policies, procedures and practices across a school organisation is the start of a 'trauma responsive' process that will need reflexivity, evaluation and fine-tuning. Training may include emotion coaching and trauma-sensitive classroom practices with an emphasis on language and restorative responses to behaviour in order to de-escalate and empower, as opposed to escalating and re-traumatising children and young people. A school organisation will be truly 'trauma-informed' when these values, principles and actions become embedded in the culture of the school.

The National Institute for Health and Care Excellence (NICE, 2015) supports incorporating attachment and trauma-informed programmes at a whole-school level and training administrators, teachers and staff to better respond to the socio-emotional, behavioural and academic challenges faced by children and young people. In England, one in six children and young people has reported having mental health issues (NHS England, 2020) indicating the need for more targeted support for all children. Schools and FE colleges have been instructed to act independently and implement their own trauma-informed and or mental health support programmes for students in colleges and schools (Cortina et al., 2021). Universities provide mental health support and services to students, however, few have adapted to trauma-informed policies.

There is a wide variety of trauma-informed resources available to schools developed by the medical, mental health, research, policy/advocacy and social service fields. As trauma-informed school programmes are in their infancy in the UK and other parts of the world, more empirical research is sought to identify the strengths and challenges of these programmes and grow the evidence base. However, after a review of research on the effectiveness of trauma-informed school programmes in the UK, evidence suggests that the key areas of improvements in the early stages experienced by schools, and discussed in more detail below, are:

- A greater understanding of students' challenges
- Improved student learning and emotional wellbeing
- Greater confidence and ability to address young people's adverse behaviours
- Reduced exclusions
- Effective programme implementation with a whole-school approach and committed leadership.

More specifically, evaluations of the following school programmes in the UK appear promising. These studies are not all inclusive but, rather, represent a sample of the empirical research studies examining the impact of trauma-informed approaches on both student and school outcomes:

- A preliminary evaluation of 300 schools participating in the Alex Timpson Attachment and Trauma Programme showed that teachers were more effective in supporting vulnerable young people through emotional coaching and restorative practices because teachers understood student behaviour from an attachment, trauma and biopsychological perspective (Harrison, 2022). More than a third of the schools reported that 'the training had a positive impact on vulnerable children's engagement (97.4%), learning (92.0%), attainment (78.6%) and attendance (71.5%), as well as reducing the use of sanctions (81.2%)' (Timpson Review, 2022).

- A study in Wales that evaluated the impact of attachment awareness training on 64 educators in 4 pupil referral units found that teachers felt more confident, aware and skilled to work with vulnerable youth with improved communication (Greenhalgh et al., 2020).
- An attachment aware schools programme involving 77 schools in Derbyshire County between 2015 and 2019 found a positive shift in the school ethos, improved pedagogical practices and outcomes in learning and students' emotional wellbeing (Kelly et al., 2020).
- The Attachment Aware Schools (AAS) \Project involving 40 schools in two different local authorities within the UK found that students improved academically in reading, writing and maths. Behaviourally, fewer students were excluded or faced negative repercussions. Educators and staff reported a greater ability to manage their own emotions and more confidence in addressing the emotions of students as a result of emotion coaching training (Rose et al., 2019).
- An evaluation of the Leicestershire Virtual School's Attachment Aware Schools Programme after training on attachment and trauma and emotional coaching to 24 schools found that senior leader commitment and support were vital to implementing a whole-school approach and aligning school principles throughout administrations, teachers and staff. Preliminary findings pointed to improved teacher-student relationships and student wellbeing as a result of enhanced confidence, knowledge, skills and attitudes when engaging with vulnerable young people (Fancourt and Sebba, 2018).

I would like to close this chapter by urging caution. There is a fine line between trauma awareness and ensuring that a child's aspiration and capability is not squashed because 'they are dealing with trauma'. This is not an easy tightrope to walk, but in my conversations with many adults over the years, academically and anecdotally, education has been their way out, their reason for living and, often, their escape. I have heard far too many times that knowledge about trauma and adversity has been interpreted as reductive. We must never reduce anyone to their trauma but rather seek to understand that it has had an impact. The relational connection that you provide might be a seed, a root or a branch that makes all the difference.

Summary

This chapter has sought to substantiate the importance of developing trauma-informed settings whether in education settings or any other settings in which children and young people reside.

I have argued that belonging is an antidote to trauma and that therefore embedding a trauma-informed culture is central to cultivating belonging. Even against the backdrop of a rising number of children coming into care, the impact of a global pandemic, the rise of children living in poverty and the mental health and wellbeing distress shown in children and young people, there is hope and there is a way of working that can fundamentally make a difference for children and young people. Understanding Attachment Theory provides a popular and straightforward way of categorising behaviours. However, it needs to be understood that attachment needs and behaviour are flexible across the life course because we never lose our need for attachment and belonging in meaningful relationships. Contemporary knowledge suggests a level of complexity that simply was not available previously, which in turn reflects an increasingly complex world. The insertion of neuroscientific knowledge in child development, the extensive literature on the impact and legacy of trauma coupled with a deeper understanding of the resources and conditions that help humans thrive highlight that the relationship between attachment and belonging has become a more complex one.

Key Chapter Takeaways

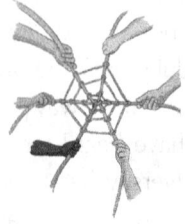

- This chapter provides a valuable supposition that having a sense of belonging is impacted by attachment relationships and is of fundamental human importance across the life course. Human needs vary, are interrelated and contextualised and are experienced differently depending on factors such as age, culture, gender and race.
- Education and children's social care are deeply interwoven, despite being treated as separate sectors.
- Administrative data captures a moment in time and lacks the nuance of individual experiences. Outcomes vary widely based on age, experiences, relational opportunities and access to education.
- Education plays a crucial role in enhancing the trajectories of care-experienced individuals. Ensuring access to education at critical developmental stages is crucial.

Reflection

How can understanding the historical context of marginalised and disadvantaged groups influence your approach to supporting children in care within your practice? How can you be more mindful of the language you use to avoid stigmatisation and promote a positive identity for children in care? Which piece of research in this chapter could you share with colleagues? How might it shape your practice?

References and Bibliography

Adoption UK. (2017). Adoption UK'S Schools & Exclusions Report. Retrieved 23 July 2024 from https://production.basw.co.uk/sites/default/files/resources/basw_45038-5.pdf

Allen, K. A. (2021). *The Psychology of Belonging.* London: Routledge.

Anda, R. F., Felitti, V. J., Bremner, J. D., Walker, J. D., Whitfield, C., Perry, B. D., Dube, S. R., & Giles, W. H. (2006). The enduring effects of abuse and related adverse experiences in childhood. A convergence of evidence from neurobiology and epidemiology. *European Archives of Psychiatry and Clinical Neuroscience,* 256(3): 174–186. https://doi.org/10.1007/s00406-005-0624-4

Antonsich, M. (2010). Searching for belonging – an analytical framework. *Geography Compass,* 4(6): 644–659.

Ashford, R. D., Brown, A. M., McDaniel, J., & Curtis, B. (2019). Biased labels: an experimental study of language and stigma among individuals in recovery and health professionals. *Substance Use & Misuse,* 54(8): 1376–1384.

Barnardo's. (2020). Barnardo's declares 'state of emergency' as number of children needing foster care during Coronavirus pandemic rises by 44%. Retrieved on 10 January 2024 from https://www.barnardos.org.uk/news/children-need-barnardos-fostering-services-more-half-during-coronavirus-pandemic

Barnardo's. (2021). No Place Like Home. Retrieved on 9 August 2023 from https://www.barnardos.org.uk/research/no-place-like-home-experiences-leaving-care-system

Baumeister, R., & Leary, M. (1995). The need to belong: desire for interpersonal attachments as a fundamental human motivation. *Psychological Bulletin,* 117(3): 497–529. https://doi.org/10.1037/0033-2909.117.3.497

Bennett, D. L., Schlüter, D. K., Melis, G., Bywaters, P., Alexiou, A., Barr, B., Wickham, S., & Taylor-Robinson, D. (2022). Child poverty and children entering care in England, 2015–20: a longitudinal ecological study at the local area level. *The Lancet. Public Health,* 7(6): e496–e503. https://doi .org/10.1016/S2468-2667(22)00065-2

Berger, E., & Martin, K. (2021). Embedding trauma-informed practice within the education sector. *Journal of Community & Applied Social Psychology,* 31(2): 223–227. https://doi.org/10.1002/casp.2494

Bouzenita, A. I., & Boulanouar, A. W. (2016). Maslow's Hierarchy of Needs: an Islamic critique. *Intellectual Discourse,* 24(1): 59–81.

Bronfenbrenner, U. (1979). *The Ecology of Human Development; Experiments by Nature and Design.* Cambridge, MA: Harvard University Press.

Care Leavers Association. (2019). Effectively abandoned – care leavers in the criminal justice system. Retrieved on 23 May 2023 from https://www .careleavers.com/wp- content/uploads/2022/05/CJS-Report-2019-edit.pdf

Cherry, L. (2023). *The Brightness of Stars; Stories from Care Experienced Adults to Inspire Change* (3rd ed.). Abingdon: Routledge.

Chimange, M., & Bond, S. (2020). Strategies used by child and youth care workers in to develop belonging and foster healthy attachments with young people in care in child and youth care centers in Tshwane, South Africa. *Children and Youth Services Review,* 118

Condliffe, E. (2023). 'Out of sight, out of mind': an interpretative phenomenological analysis of young people's experience of isolation rooms/booths in UK mainstream secondary schools. *Emotional and Behavioural Difficulties,* 28(4): 1–16.

Cooper, V. & Whyte, D. (Eds.). (2017). *The Violence of Austerity.* Pluto Press.

Corless, C. (2021). *Belonging. A Memoir of Place, Beginnings and One Woman's Search for Truth and Justice for the Tuam Babies.* Dublin: Hachette Books Ireland.

Corrales, T., Waterford, M., Goodwin-Smith, I., Wood, L., Yourell, T., & Ho, C. (2016). Childhood adversity, sense of belonging and psychosocial outcomes in emerging adulthood: a test of mediated pathways. *Children and Youth Services Review,* 63, 110–119.

Cortina, M., Linehan, T., & Sheppard, K. (2021) *Working towards Mentally Healthy Schools and FE Colleges: The Voice of Students.* London: Anna Freud National Centre for Children and Families.

Cox, P., Shore, H,, Alker, Z, & Godfrey, B. (2018). Tracking the gendered life courses of care leavers in 19th century Britain. *Longitudinal and Life Course Studies: International Journal,* 9 (1): 115–128.

Crittenden, P. (2006). A Dynamic-Maturational Model of Attachment. *Australian and New Zealand Journal of Family Therapy, 27.*

Daniels, H., Thompson, I., Porter, J., Tawell, A. & Emery, H. (2020). School exclusion risks after COVID-19. Retrieved on 23 July 2024 from https://www.education.ox.ac.uk/wp-content/uploads/2019/11/Daniels-et-al.-2020_School-Exclusion-Risks-after-COVID-19.pdf

Demie, F. (2021). The experience of black Caribbean pupils in school exclusion in England. *Educational Review (Birmingham),* 73(1): 55–70.

Department for Education (DfE). (2020). *Permanent and Fixed Period Exclusions in England 2018 to 2019.* London: Department for Education.

Department for Education (DfE). (2022). *Keeping Children Safe in Education: Statutory Guidance for Schools and Colleges.* Retrieved on 23 July 2024 from https://assets.publishing.service.gov.uk/media/64f0a68ea78c5f0 00dc6f3b2/Keeping_children_safe_in_education_2023.pdf

Department for Education (DfE). (2024). *Main Findings: Children's Social Care in England 2024.* Retrieved on 21 July 2024 from https://www.gov.uk/government/statistics/childrens-social-care-in-england-2024/main-findings-childrens-social-care-in-england-2024

Department for Education (DfE). (2024). *Children Looked After in England Including Adoptions.* Retrieved on 21 July 2024 from https://explore-education-statistics.service.gov.uk/find-statistics/children-looked-after-in-england-including-adoptions

Department for Education (DfE), Home Office & Ministry of Justice (DfE, HO & MoJ). (2018). *The National Protocol on Reducing Unnecessary Criminalisation of Looked After Children and Care Leavers.* Retrieved on 10 July 2019 from https://assets.publishing.service.gov.uk/government/uploads/system/uploads/attachment_daa/file/765082/The_national_protocol_on_reducing_unnecessary_criminalisation_of_looked-after_children_and_care_.pdf

Eagleman, D. (2021). *Livewired: The Inside Story of the Ever-changing Brain.* Edinburgh: Pantheon Books.

Fancourt, N., & Sebba, J. (2018). The Leicestershire Virtual School's Attachment Aware Schools Programme: Evaluation Report. REES Centre. Retrieved on 22 July 2024 from https://www.education.ox.ac.uk/wp-content/uploads/2019/05/Leicestershire-Attachment-Aware-Schools-Programme-Evaluation-Report.pdf

Felitti V. J., Anda, R. F., Nordenberg, D., Williamson, D. F., Spitz, A. M., Edwards, V., Koss, M. P., & Marks, J. S. (1998). Relationship of childhood abuse and household dysfunction to many of the leading causes of death in adults. The Adverse Childhood Experiences (ACEs) Study. *American Journal of Preventive Medicine,* 14 (4): 245–258.

Fuller, M. (2019). *A Search for Belonging.* London: Bonnier Books UK.

Gerhardt, S. (2015). *Why Love Matters: How Affection Shapes a Baby's Brain* (2nd ed.). New York: Taylor & Francis.

Golding, K. S. (2020). Understanding and helping children who have experienced maltreatment. *Paediatrics and Child Health,* 30(11): 371–377.

Goodenow, C., & Grady, K. (1993). The relationship of school belonging and friends' values to academic motivation among urban adolescent students. *The Journal of Experimental Education,* 62(1): 60–71.

Greenhalgh, R., Fflur, S., Donnelly, K., Kirkaldie, H., & McDonnell, L. (2020). An evaluation of the impact of attachment and trauma training for pupil referral unit staff. *Developmental Child Welfare,* 2(2): 75–91.

Harris, M., & Fallot, R.D. (2001). Envisioning a trauma-informed service system: a vital paradigm shift. *New Directions for Ment Health Services,* (89): 3–22.

Harrison, N. (2022). *Attachment and Trauma Awareness Training: Headteachers' Perspectives on the Impact on Vulnerable Children, Staff and the School.* REES Centre. Retrieved on 23 July 2024 from https://www.education.ox.ac.uk/wp-content/uploads/2019/05/Timpson-working-paper-5.pdf

Harrison, N., Baker, Z., & Stevenson, J. (2022). Employment and further study outcomes for care-experienced graduates in the UK. *Higher Education,* 83, 357–378 https://doi.org/10.1007/s10734-020-00660-w

Hart, H., & Rubia, K. (2012). Neuroimaging of child abuse: a critical review. *Frontiers in Human Neuroscience,* 6: 52. https://doi.org/10.3389/fnhum.2012.00052

Hofstede, G. (1984). The cultural relativity of the quality of life concept. *Academy of Management Review,* 9(3): 389–398.

hooks, b. (2009). *Belonging. A Culture of Place.* New York: Routledge.

Jackson, S. (1987). *The Education of Children in Care.* Bristol: School of Applied Social Studies, University of Bristol.

Jones, L., Dean, C., Dunhill, A., Hope, M. A., & Shaw, P. A. (2020). 'We are the same as everyone else just with a different and unique backstory': identity, belonging and 'othering' within education for young people who are 'looked after'. *Children and Society,* 34: 492–506.

Kelly, P., Watt, L., & Giddens, S. (2020). An attachment aware schools programme: a safe space, a nurturing learning community. *Pastoral Care in Education,* 38(4): 335–354. https://doi.org/10.1080/02643944.2020.1751685

Kishimi, I., & Koga, F. (2019). *The Courage to Be Disliked: How to Free Yourself, Change Your Life and Achieve Real Happiness.* Allen & Unwin.

Lopez Lopez, M., Gonzalez, A., Victor, R., Ten Brummelaar, M., Van, M., Kevin, R. O., Wielaaijer-Vincent, L., Gonzalez Alvarez, V., Howard, E., Mallon, G., Orwa, S., Pierzchawka, N., Ridderbos, B., Ros, C., Torsius S., Wijkstra, S., & Verwer, D.,(2021). *Working with LGBTQIA Youth in the Child Welfare System: Perspectives from Youth and Professionals.* Groningen: University of Groningen Press.

Main, M., & Solomon, J. (1986). Discovery of an insecure-disorganized/ disoriented attachment pattern. In T. B. Brazelton and M. W. Yogman (Eds.), *Affective Development in Infancy.* Norwood: Ablex.

Martin-Denham, S. (2020). Riding the rollercoaster of school exclusion coupled with drug misuse: the lived experience of caregivers. *Emotional and Behavioural Difficulties,* 25(3–4), 244–263.

Maslow, A. H. (1943). A theory of human motivation. *Psychological Review,* 50(4): 370.

Maslow, A. H. (1968). *Toward a Psychology of Being.* New York: D. Van Nostrand.

Maslow, A. H. (1971). *The Farther Reaches of Human Nature.* New York: The Viking Press.

Morgan, F., & Costello, E. (2022). *Square Pegs* (I. Gilbert, Ed.). Independent Thinking Press.

Ministry of Justice. (2018). https://wp.lancs.ac.uk/care-custody/files/2019/10/ CareCustodyLiteratureReview.pdf

Mittelman, W. (1991). Maslow's study of self-actualization: a reinterpretation. *Journal of Humanistic Psychology,* 31(1): 114–135. https://doi.org/10.1177 /0022167891311010

National Collaborating Centre for Mental Health (UK). (2015). Children's attachment: attachment in children and young people who are adopted from care, in care or at high risk of going into care. London: National Institute for Health and Care Excellence (NICE); Nov. (NICE Guideline, No. 26.) Retrieved on 23 July 2024 from https://www.ncbi.nlm.nih.gov/books /NBK338143

National Health Service (NHS). (2020). *Mental Health of Children and Young People in England, 2020: Wave 1 Follow Up to the 2017 Survey.*

Retrieved on 22 July 2024 from https://digital.nhs.uk/data-and-information /publications/statistical/mental-health-of-children-and-young-people-in -england/2020-wave-1-follow-up#

National Society for the Prevention of Cruelty to Children (NSPCC). (2023). Why language matters: why you should avoid the acronym 'LAC' when talking about children in care. Retrieved on 21 November 2023 from https://learning.nspcc.org.uk/news/why-language-matters/looked-after -children

O'Donohue, J. (1998). *Exploring Our Hunger to Belong.* London: Bantam Books.

Office for National Statistics. (2022). *The Education Background of Looked-after Children Who Interact with the Criminal Justice System.* Retrieved on 9 August 2023 from https://www.ons.gov.uk/peoplepopulationand community/educationandchildcare/articles/thee ducationbackgroundof lookedafterchildrenwhointeractwiththecriminaljusticesystem/december 2022

O'Higgins, A., Sebba, J., & Gardner, F. (2017). What are the factors associated with educational achievement for children in kinship or foster care?: A systematic review. *Children and Youth Services Review,* 79: 198–220.

Parker, E. (2017). An Actor-Network Theory reading of change for children in public care. *British Educational Research Journal,* 43(1): 151–167.

Perry, B. D. (2006). Applying principles of neurodevelopment to clinical work with maltreated and traumatized children: the neurosequential model of therapeutics. In N. B. Webb (Ed.), *Working with Traumatized Youth in Child Welfare.* The Guilford Press.

Perry, B. (2019). Relational poverty. Word on the streets. Retrieved on 23 July 2024 from https://www.wordonthestreets.net/Articles/610528/Relational _poverty.aspx

Porges, S. (2011). *The Polyvagal Theory: Neurophysiological Foundations of Emotions, Attachment, Communication, and Self-regulation.* New York: W. W. Norton and Company.

Power, S., & Taylor, C. (2020). Not in the classroom, but still on the register: hidden forms of school exclusion. *International Journal of Inclusive Education,* 24(8): 867–881.

Reisz, S., Duschinsky, R., & Siegel, D. J. (2018). Disorganized attachment and defence: exploring John Bowlby's unpublished reflections. *Attachment Human Development,* 20(2): 107–134.

Riley, K. (2022). *Compassionate Leadership for School Belonging.* London: University College London Press.

Rogers, C. R. (1951). *Client-centred Therapy; Its Current Practice, Implications and Theory.* Boston, MA: Houghton Mifflin.

Rojas, M., Méndez, A., & Watkins-Fassler, K. (2023). The hierarchy of needs empirical examination of Maslow's theory and lessons for development. *World Development, 165,* https://doi.org/10.1016/j.worlddev.2023.106185

Rose, J., McGuire-Snieckus, R., Gilbert, L., & McInnes, K. (2019). Attachment aware schools: the impact of a targeted and collaborative intervention. *Pastoral Care in Education,* 37(2): 162–184. https://doi.org/10.1080/02643944.2019.1625429

Röttger-Rössler, B. (2014). Bonding and belonging beyond WEIRD worlds: rethinking attachment theory on the basis of cross-cultural anthropological data. In H. Otto & H. Keller (Eds.), *Different Faces of Attachment: Cultural Variations on a Universal Human Need.* Cambridge: Cambridge University Press. https://doi.org/10.1017/CBO9781139226684.009

Schore, A. (2001). The effects of early relational trauma on right brain development, affect regulation, and infant mental health. *Infant Mental Health Journal,* 22(1–2): 201–269.

Scottish Government. (2020). *The Promise Scotland.* Retrieved on 9 May 2023 from https://thepromise.scot/what-is-the-promise/about

Sebba, J., Berridge, D., Luke, N., Fletcher, J., Bell, K., Strand, S., Thomas, S., Sinclair, I., & O'Higgins, A. (2015). The educational progress of looked after children in England: linking care and educational data. In REES Centre Reports. University of Oxford Department of Education/University of Bristol.

Shonkoff, J., & Garner, A. (2012). The lifelong effects of early childhood adversity and toxic stress. *Pediatrics,* 129(1): e232–246.

Siegel, D. J. (2010). *Mindsight.* Oneworld Publications.

Siegel, D. J., & Bryson T. P. (2020). *The Power of Showing Up: How Parental Presence Shapes Who Our Kids Become and How Their Brains Get Wired (First).* Ballantine Books.

Smith, M., Cameron, C., & Reimer, D. (2017). From attachment to recognition for children in care. *British Journal of Social Work,* 47: 1606–1623.

Sprince, J. (2015). From owning to belonging. In *Towards Belonging* (1st ed.). Routledge. https://doi.org/10.4324/9780429484117-6

Substance Abuse and Mental Health Services Administration (SAMHSA). (2014). *SAMHSA's Concept of Trauma and Guidance for a Trauma-Informed Approach.* HHS Publication No. (SMA) 14-4884. Rockville, MD: Substance Abuse and Mental Health Services Administration, 2014.

Teicher, M. H., Samson, J. A., Anderson, C. M., & Ohashi, K. (2016). The effects of childhood maltreatment on brain structure, function and connectivity. *Nature Reviews. Neuroscience*, 17(10): 652–666. https://doi .org/10.1038/nrn.2016.111

Thapar, C. (2021). *Cut Short: Youth Violence, Loss and Hope in the City.* Penguin Books.

The Adolescent and Children's Trust (TACT). (2019). Language that cares. Retrieved on 19 June 2023 from https://www.tactcare.org.uk/content/ uploads/2019/03/TACT-Language-that-cares-2019_online.pdf

The LACGro Project. (2021). *The Lifelong Health and Wellbeing Trajectories of People who Have Been in Care.* Retrieved on 9 May 2023 from https:// www.nuffieldfoundation.org/wp-   content/uploads/2021/07/The-lifelon g-health-and-wellbeing-trajectories-of-people-who-have-   been-in-care .pdf

The National Child Traumatic Stress Network (NCTSN). (2021) *All NCTSN Resources.* Retrieved on 23 July 2024 from https://www.nctsn.org/ resources/all-nctsn-resources

The Voice Project. (2021). Language that cares. Retrieved on 23 July 2024 from   https://www.staffordshire.gov.uk/Care-for-children-and-families/ Lookedafterchildren/thechildrenyoungpeoplesvoiceproject.aspx

Thomas, M. S., Crosby, S., & Vanderhaar, J. (2019). Trauma-informed practices in schools across two decades: an interdisciplinary review of research. *Review of Research in Education,* 43(1): 422–452. https://doi.org/10.3102 /0091732X18821123

Timpson Review. (2022). https://www.aati-reescentre.education.ox.ac.uk/wp -content/uploads/2022/07/AATI-report_2022.pd

Treisman, K. (2017). *Working with Relational and Developmental Trauma in Children and Adolescents.* Abingdon: Routledge.

Treisman, K. (2021). *A Treasure Box for Creating Trauma-informed Organizations: A Ready-to-use Resource for Trauma, Adversity, And Culturally Informed, Infused and Responsive Systems.* London: Jessica Kingsley Publishers.

Tyler, I. (2020). *Stigma: The Machinery of Inequality* (1st ed.). London.

Van der Kolk, B. (2015). *The Body Keeps the Score: Brain, Mind, and Body in the Healing of Trauma.* New York: Penguin.

Virdee, S., & McGeever, B. (2018). Racism, crisis, Brexit. *Ethnic and Racial Studies,* 41(10): 1802–1819.

Voss, P., Thomas, M. E., Cisneros-Franco, J. M., & de Villers-Sidani, É. (2017). Dynamic brains and the changing rules of neuroplasticity: implications for learning and recovery. *Frontiers in Psychology*, 8: 1657.

Webber, L. (2017). A school's journey in creating a relational environment which supports attachment and emotional security. *Emotional and Behavioural Difficulties*, 22(4): 317–331.

Wilkerson S. R. (2010). Another day older and deeper in therapy: can the dynamicmaturational model offer a way out?: Attachment, children and families: The DynamicMaturational Model. *Clinical Child Psychology and Psychiatry*, 15(3): 423–432.

Wright, S. (2015). More-than-human, emergent belongings: a weak theory approach. *Progress in Human Geography*, 39(4): 391–411.

Younge, G. (2017). The cause of death that dare not speak its name: austerity. Retrieved on 10 January 2024 from https://www.theguardian.com/membership/commentisfree/2017/apr/15/knife-crime-cause-death-dare-not-speak-name-austerity-cuts-youth-funding

PART TWO:
Reconceptualising Weaving the Web: Contemporary Opportunities to Weave

5
Language That Heals

Introduction

In Part One, I brought you myself, from where I stand and what I bring, arguing that whether we are explicit about it or not, we ultimately bring ourselves in all our glory into our work with those we seek to help and support. I also weaved meaning from my participant's experiences to consider what it means to others. I then ventured into the historical context that has formed and shaped our services for children and young people and suggested that it has cast a long shadow with its presence still felt in current times. I demonstrated how stigmatisation weaves its way into legislation, into professional parlance and, ultimately, into the shaping and forming of children and young people's identities. Finally, unbelonging and its lasting legacy was explored.

In Part Two, the invitation is to think about what opportunities we have available to us right now so that we can create the change needed to develop the foundations for weaving belonging into our work. In this chapter, we're going to start with deconstructing the language we use in order to change it. We see the world through the language we use and it is only by changing our language that we will change how we work.

Historical Overview

In Chapter 3, we began the journey of looking at language and labelling and how that adds fuel to the fire of stigma. Language helps us

DOI: 10.4324/9781003426592-8

make sense of our experiences and how we might communicate them to others. The world we inhabit is interpreted through language and how we transmit culture or cultures. When thinking about the children's services and the education system, we might consider them to be different cultures to make sense of independently. They are different sectors with their own images, signs and symbols (language) that young people attempt to navigate. Because of the nature of my research, which sought to make sense of how those who were in care as children and also excluded from school made sense of belonging, the participants' experience of these systems spanned several decades. Making sense of that social and political landscape across the different decades that a person may have been in care and lived after care is complex. This exploration involved thinking historically about language, identity and belonging, and observing the different legislation that applied at the time. Those different decades played out against the backdrop of different legislation, societal views and ways of understanding human distress. This can be seen most clearly in the language used. You might be aware that The Children's Society which was founded in 1881 was called the Church of England Incorporated Society for Providing Homes for Waifs and Strays. Waifs and strays! Lest we forget that the child with special educational needs was once the 'educationally subnormal' child and the child now labelled with social, mental and emotional health needs was once considered 'maladjusted'.

A historical overview of all the language used to describe children, young people and their families in contact with those who have taken an interest in their welfare is beyond the scope of this book and a huge research project all of its own. However, we can draw on enough examples to educate ourselves in the power of language, its relationship to unbelonging and stigma and how that impacts a person's identity and understanding of themselves. The parents and the children of those exposed to circumstances that bring about poverty have consistently endured language that harms. The uniformed 'paupers' and the 'inmates' of the workhouses where families were separated and the schedule was gruelling were expected to be grateful for being 'housed'.

The concept of the deserving poor and the undeserving poor arose from the Poor Law 1834. Today, the notion of the deserving and undeserving poor lingers but the language has shifted to 'skiver' and 'work-shy' (undeserving) endlessly pitted against those considered to be 'hard-working families' who are doing several jobs but still may not be managing (deserving). Who decides who is deserving and who is not remains a dance between government policy and social attitudes, both working together seeking to anticipate the mood of the other and both with different agendas!

Importance of Language

When it comes to children and young people who come into contact with services, the language used adopts phrases like: 'hard to reach', 'looked-after child', 'child in need', 'excluded', 'won't engage' developed from legislation and professional 'speak'. This language creates a narrative and before you know it, a child who is meeting their family, describes the meeting as 'contact'! By using different language, there is an opportunity to form a different narrative, a different way of understanding experiences, a different way of thinking about what it means to be someone who uses services. Not children as the waifs and strays of the 19th century, but children who have a right to belong in their community, in some sort of family where they are protected.

We must be curious about where the word 'belonging' is and isn't included in legislation as this directly influences our work. Cultivating belonging in education and in services working with children in care is referred to directly in other countries but hardly ever found in the UK. For example, the concept of belonging can be found in *The Early Years Learning Framework* for Australia (2022) which is titled 'Belonging, Being and Becoming. and mentions the word 'belonging' 82 times. Similarly, in Alberta, Canada, the early years and care framework makes reference to belonging' throughout (Makovichuk et al., 2014). This international policy suggests that practice in international sectors such as education may be clearer about how exclusion is a feature of the experience of being in care and being excluded from school, and therefore that cultivating belonging might be a helpful solution. Learning about belonging in policy internationally led to an exploration of policy across the UK and the devolved nations, commencing with looking through documents released from the Department of Education that act as Guidance, Statutory Guidance and Statutory Frameworks. Out of eight key documents (see below) that are relevant, one document mentioned belonging once and another document mentioned belonging twice. The rest did not feature the word belonging. This legislation is applicable from the beginning of life, nevertheless the evidence and research that we have available to us about the importance of the early years in childhood development reveals that the concept of belonging was overwhelmingly absent.

My observation is that the language of legislation becomes the language of professionals which subsequently seeps into the language of children and young people. Imagine then if 'belonging' became part of the language included in policy and legislation; that too could seep into the internal narrative of our children and young people.

> Imagine ... When practitioners change the language used between them, when record keeping is done in such a way that they [professionals] understand that the adult that the child once was can gain healing from the writing, this will directly serve to reduce some of the impact of stigma and how identity is shaped in the developing years.

If we are serious about changing the cultures that influence the places and spaces utilised by young people and being able to cultivate belonging, then the language used needs a complete deconstruction. Such a deconstruction would move us far away from problematising

Table 5.1   Documents on Guidance, Statutory Guidance and Statutory Frameworks

	Document	Number of pages	Number of times 'exclusion' mentioned	Number of times 'belonging' mentioned	Number of times 'relationship' mentioned
Doc 1	*The Best Start for Life: A Vision for the 1,001 Critical Days, The Early Years Healthy Development Review Report (HM Govt, 2021)*	147	6	0	22
Doc 2	*Statutory Framework for the Early Years Foundation Stage: Setting the Standards for Learning, Development and Care for Children from Birth to Five (DfE, 2021)*	53	0	0	9
Doc 3	*Keeping Children Safe in Education: Statutory Guidance for Schools and Colleges (DfE, 2020)*	179	7	0	0
Doc 4	*Exclusion from Maintained Schools, Academies and Pupil Referral Units in England: Statutory Guidance for Those with Legal Responsibilities in Relation to Exclusion (DfE, 2017)*	62	288	0	0

(Continued)

Table 5.1 (Continued)

	Document	Number of pages	Number of times 'exclusion' mentioned	Number of times 'belonging' mentioned	Number of times 'relationship' mentioned
Doc 5	Suspension and Permanent Exclusion from Maintained Schools, Academies and Pupil Referral Units in England, Including Pupil Movement Guidance for Maintained Schools, Academies, and Pupil Referral Units in England (DfE, 2022) Updated version of Doc 1	72	223	1	0
Doc 6	The Designated Teacher for Looked-after and Previously Looked-after Children: Statutory Guidance on Their Roles and Responsibilities (DfE, 2018)	50	26	0	14
Doc 7	Special Educational Needs and Disabilities (SEND) and Alternative Provision (AP) Improvement Plan (DfE, 2023)	101	3	2	9
Doc 8	Behaviour in Schools. Advice for Headteachers and School Staff (DfE, 2024)	34	13	0	6

the child, and instead move us towards a language that enables children and young people to understand that they are accepted just as they are. Acceptance is one of the roots of belonging.

However, on a positive note, there are some recent changes in policy in England which suggests the disconnect between research, international policy and policy in the UK on the issue of belonging may well be turning. One reference to belonging has recently emerged in the Children's Social Care Reform in the section on Kinship Carers (DfE, 2023a). Kinship Carers are close family members or friends of family members. Although the word 'love' is in the title of the document (*Children's Social Care: Stable Homes, Built on Love Consultation Response*, DfE, 2023b) and is mentioned a further 42 times throughout, the word 'belonging' is also mentioned (DfE, 2023b, p. 39). The word belonging only has a sole mention, but it potentially indicates a turning point for policy and, therefore, for practice too.

However, it is professional practice that has influenced the introduction of belonging into policy. Local strategies are already incorporating belonging in their plans. It is worth highlighting that Bristol's Strategy (*Bristol Belonging Strategy: Belonging from the Beginning 2021–2024*) makes it clear that belonging is key to thinking about the 0–5 age group of children (Bristol City Council, 2021). Dorset's 10-year strategy plan for children, young people and families has also acknowledged that belonging is key, by developing a Belonging Strategy in education (Dorset Council, 2023).

Let's Take A Moment …

Hopefully, you're now thinking about your own use of language. In the words of Maya Angelou, 'when we know better, we do better'. Go gently. (I'll remind you of this again at the end of the chapter.)

Where Does Language Sit in Practice?

It is clear, as explored in Chapter 3, that the language used in policy is neither consistently nor thoughtfully used across settings and services, which opens up a pathway to using problematic terminology in day-to-day interactions with children. The terminology of this language is also expressed in children's 'files' which will be available to them as adults. Furthermore, outdated language may linger for a long time after that particular policy language has changed, showing up as ongoing public opinion. But this language has an impact on how children and young people and the adults they become feel about themselves. Children's homes were called residential units during my time in one in the 1980s, and it required a deliberate effort to change the terms we used. Shifting our language requires us to be committed to change through self awareness, curiosity, cultural humility and action.

Moving on to building an identity in the developing years, it is important to understand that children who are in care are exposed to a number of adults, far more than a child outside of this system! This is often, in my experience, incredibly misunderstood. From a strengths based view, the exposure can create a real capacity for dealing with different types of people, an ability to adjust, a mechanism for 'tuning

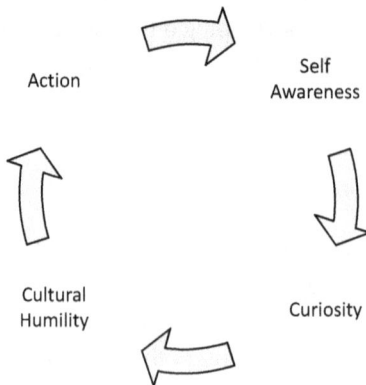

Action   Self Awareness

Cultural Humility   Curiosity

Figure 5.1   Intentional Change

in' to a variety of people. Taking a different approach, it can make shaping and forming identity more challenging. Where do I belong? Who are you to me? How long will you be here? Can I see me in you?

Staying with the idea of 'practitioner or professional speak', there are so many examples of terms about which we should try to raise awareness. For example, the use of the term 'contact' to describe a meeting with family members or 'respite' to refer to foster carers taking a break. We might also think about terminology such as 'birth parents' to mean parents or 'in care' to mean living away from home or 'place-ment' to mean where the child lives. Those to whom children in care are exposed come from many walks of life in a way that children liv-ing in their families are not, each with their own unique relationship to the world. Children in the care system may have had several social workers, several foster carers and a number of people living in and around the family, possibly residential workers, while also attending several different schools. They will also have an independent review-ing officer, a school nurse, someone assigned to them from the virtual school and potentially someone from the Children Adolescent Mental Health Services (CAMHS), all bringing their different agendas, motiva-tions and perspectives to the child. These relationships are paid ones where people can leave, take holidays or be off sick. This exposure is quite unique to the care experience.

Meaning making of all these diverse types of relationships within the context of making sense of belonging and how that is understood is central to this book. Through my practice, I have seen first hand just how multi-faceted, multi-layered and interdisciplinary language is (Cherry, 2022). My doctoral research provided me with the opportu-nity to analyse language used by participants so that I could garner a more profound understanding of the impact that language had on them. The professionalisation of language regarding deeply challeng-ing interpersonal experiences, the language from policy and how this language enters a person's lexicon which shapes personal identity were so often internalised by participants.

Peppered throughout the wisdom collected in my research, terms such as 'maladaptive', 'difficult child', 'problem child' and 'naughty boys' were adopted to describe children. This located the problem within the child or young person, while inadvertently shaping an identity that would last far longer than the service used.

It is common in professional conversations in meetings to hear 'problem children' described as 'hard to reach' or 'difficult to engage,' or as having 'challenging behaviour'. In these contexts, there are 'cases' and 'risk assessments' and 'contact'. All these terminologies place the problem on the child and serve to detach them from connection or belonging with others. As stated earlier in this book, this disconnection can sever any hope of creating a sense of belonging and has a history that was very deliberate in its intention. Examples of this range from the Foundling Hospital changing babies' names to ones that had no connection to their birth family, to what was known as an illegitimate child being known as *filius nullius* meaning 'nobody's child' (Williams, 2018). There is every reason to argue that language continues to harm children. This can be seen in services and settings who work with children in care, thus supporting current research on the connection between language and how it interplays with stigma and injustice in relation to children in care (Fieller and Loughlin, 2022). Such research runs in parallel with co-produced projects on language undertaken by organisations working with children and young people in care (TACT, 2019; Coram Voice, 2020; NSPCC, 2023).

The research provides concrete evidence that the effects of language used can, and does, span across the life course. This connection between the use of professionalised language and further stigma and discrimination creates a multi-layered and complex way of making sense of the self for the adult that the child in care and/or excluded from school becomes. This complexity is taken to the next level when children in care and/or excluded children work in the very setting or services that once supported them. For example, Alisha, who went on to work as a social worker, shared with me what it was like to work in that field, processing her own experiences and listening to colleagues and the way they described people:

> *I chose not to go into children's social work because of what I observed. I couldn't. I couldn't work with Professionals that were oppressive with professional mindsets that wouldn't be changed, couldn't be changed, wouldn't be challenged. So for me it was a very difficult place for me to work because I was constantly fighting and that again is another thing. Fighting as a child, fighting that oppression, fighting that discrimination to then have to do that as an adult and as a professional.*
>
> (Alisha)

Speaking in Acronyms

The current research contributes to the claim that there is a need for further interdisciplinary consideration across how language is used in the sectors of education and children's services, specifically around the overuse of acronyms such as LAC (looked after children), CIN (child in need) and SEND (special educational needs and disabilities). Furthermore, it is our duty to critically reflect on the continuous need to problematise the child or young person. We can only do this if we make space in everyday practice for writing and reflecting. Too often though we are time poor and often writing up our notes or considering how we can record things in ways that avoid acronyms or complex language is just not possible. Additionally, if those files are being written for a child with a social worker, the adult that the child becomes may want to read them. In this scenario the 'file' needs to contain language that heals not language that harms because this adult will be looking at their file to try and make sense of what happened to them. As Donna states:

> *I can tell you that I didn't know why I was there until in my late adulthood, until I read my files.*
>
> (Donna)

The overuse of acronyms persists, however:

> This language unfairly injures their right to be viewed and treated like any other child. Is this having an adverse effect on the children we care for? Most certainly, the children and young people we care for should be referred to by their name. Collectively, however, using alternatives to the words "LAC" and "children in care" would be a good start to making care more person-centred.
>
> (Fieller and Loughlin, 2022, p. 872)

Interpretation and Internalisation

Together with the complexities mentioned comes a myriad of ways to interpret meanings. This is often the case when policy becomes practice and it is internalised, understood and spoken about to others. Donna, aged 62, the oldest participant in my doctoral research, reflected on the language used in her childhood, deeming it highly inappropriate today. However, some of that terminology lingers and it certainly lingered for her. She talks about living in an 'institution', whereas Maisie who is 32, talks about a 'secure unit'. Thus, some language that we might consider as 'from the past' persists in the terminology used today, which is subsequently enacted in professional practice, and in the places and spaces within which professional practice unfolds. Moreover, this impacts on the experience and meaning making of the participants. For example, James talked about being sent to a setting which was for 'the maladjusted':

> *I was also going to a boarding school during the week and coming back to the children's home at the weekend and then we transferred to this new children's home I carried on in the school for maladjusted kids.*
>
> (James)

Did you notice how he speaks in the present? He is using the language of the time as a man in his late 50s. Matthew also shared how he felt he was viewed, while also feeling confused as to where this came from:

> *The teachers saw me as trouble they knew I was an underachiever and all my school reports used to say I was a lovely, likable, cheeky person but academically not gonna kind of amount to much and you know, an underachiever. I'm sure somewhere, I can't trace it now to be honest with you but I'm sure I saw the word inept.*
>
> (Matthew)

Discrimination and stigmatisation is fluid as it seeps into language, into the way a person is viewed and how they view themselves. It is written, spoken and appears in body language. It is often unseen but always 'felt'. The overuse of language used in policy entering into day-to-day communication with and around children and young people and their families is highly problematic. The participants seamlessly demonstrated that language lingers beyond historical relevance, ensuring a long legacy of words and attitudes that still remain in the system, in the person and in society which impacts identity and their sense of belonging. This language also impacts the possibility of less harmful ways of making meaning from childhood experiences. The words used are internalised by the people who are experiencing the service, and the language itself problematises the person. The person may feel they are the problem because the language locates the problem within the person. Thus, unless we are more intentional about how we use language, we will always use language that harms rather than language that heals. The challenge is, of course, to put an end to the overuse of language from policy by professionals. This is an interdisciplinary endeavour because education and children's services are not silos and are by nature interconnected. However, while an assistant director overseeing those two areas may understand this, practice 'on the ground' often does not. I've heard many teachers state 'I'm not a social worker' and sometimes social workers state 'that's not my area, that's education'. Sadly, this book doesn't provide a panacea, a magic wand to fix this. However, the current 'bridge' is the virtual school as first mentioned in Chapter 2, and in many areas of the country, this bridge is walked on and across very well by many professionals across both education and social care.

The Language of Trauma and Stigma

Two terms which require particular attention are stigma and trauma. Regarding stigma, although Manago et al. (2022) argued that 'it is now time to return to a broad theoretical account of stigma and how we can understand it', this research suggests that stigma should be thought of as located within the places that should help. Stigma is part of what Tyler (2020, p. 260) describes as 'stigma machines'. Public opinion on who should be stigmatised and how people are stigmatised affect these debates, but stigma is also inherent in the professional language, described above. As previously stated, I was surprised that stigma was not a word used by participants, but was an implicit part of their stories. Instead, terms such as 'bad kids', 'shame', 'stereotypes' and 'outcast' appeared in statements made by James, Crystal and Shaun:

> I was excluded from primary school aged 9 and sent to a boarding school for mal-adjusted kids. I cried and begged my social worker not to take me there because I knew it was where all the bad kids from my town went.
>
> (James)

The feeling of not belonging is inextricably linked with feeling unsafe and the shame of not being like others.

(Crystal)

I never really experienced true belonging during my care years. Rather, you're too aware that you're part of a system. One with negative connotations and stereotypes. It's not something you want to shout about. You have no meaningful peer groups because life is too sporadic and forever changing. You're an outcast and isolated – in school and out.

(Shaun)

Trauma, however, was a term that participants *did* use to describe themselves and their experiences. Trauma is defined in many ways but the following is very much my preferred definition: 'an experience or series of experiences and/or impacts from social conditions, that break or betray our inherent need for safety, belonging and dignity' (Haines, 2019, p. 74).

My research demonstrated how participants made sense of trauma in two interrelated ways – as understanding or recognising it, and as overcoming it to move forward. The devastation of trauma can be felt as a fundamental challenge to the self which forces meaning making of who that self was, and who that self is now (Roberts and Dutton, 2009). Consequently, there is a need to not only consider the trauma which moves people into these sectors and services, but what happens once they are in those services. This is how I understand Haines' (2019) definition of trauma on the 'social conditions', whilst also bringing in the notions of safety, belonging and dignity. Children can be frequently moved around, excluded from school, placed in unsuitable housing conditions, with poor access to nutritional food. These social conditions can ultimately create the environment that a child may find themselves in, which Maisie knows only too well:

> *The bedroom was like a bare concrete cell and there was just a crash mat on the floor like no wooden furniture to hold it up or nothing. Then you had a bed sheet and another one over the crash mat. But as time went on I was in and out a lot. They'd take the crash mat out and I'd sit on the concrete floor and often run at the walls. And you know, I was losing my mind half the time.*

> (Maisie)

By definition, trauma can be a challenging word and researchers and practitioners need to take the opportunity to reflect upon how they can work with trauma without always necessarily using that word. For some young people and adults, understanding their experiences as trauma can be helpful in recognising that what happened was not their fault. Believing that it is one's fault is largely how trauma can be made sense of, particularly when the trauma happened in childhood, with individuals often perceiving that there is something wrong with them, and they did something bad. Thus, it is difficult to say what each person might do with the word 'trauma'. What is more important is what one does with the word trauma in legislation, policy and practice. This relates to the appropriate place for the language of trauma or its limits as a conceptual term. In recognising that 'trauma' is different for different people, it would be unwise to be definitive.

A good start to working with trauma is to engage with trauma-informed practices. We need to be cautious, thoughtful and inherently understanding about what it is to work with humans, regardless of whether or not we know they have experienced trauma. If we are working in a manner which does not add to trauma, we can mitigate some of the effects of trauma by cultivating relationships that have safety, belonging and dignity. To echo Haines (2019), then we do not need to go 'trauma digging' and we do not need to throw around the word trauma.

Self-forgiveness

As Maya Angelou once said, 'when we know better, we do better' and I would add that it is our duty to always seek to know better. Ignorance is no defence if we do not ensure that we take responsibility for our learning and development. Learning and development is not simply the name of a department who sends us a list of training opportunities via email. So please note, you are engaged in taking responsibility for your learning simply by reading this book. It is likely that you purchased it yourself and it is likely that you are reading it outside your working hours. Therefore, you are seeking to know better with the desired outcome being that you will do better.

As a practitioner, you have probably talked and written in acronyms, you've potentially described someone in ways that are described above such as 'challenging' and you've possibly written terrible notes on a person who will go on to read those as an adult. I have been that practitioner. I was in my first few years of practice. I forgive myself for not knowing then what I now know. That is how life works so just know that the very act of reading this book is a gift to social change, to culture change and, ultimately, to the lives of children and young people. This book will change lives because you are a person who cares so deeply about your work that you take responsibility for knowing better, and for that we can all be grateful.

Summary

The analysis of language within children's services and education highlights an urgent need to reconsider how we communicate and comprehend the experiences of those we work with. This chapter has dived into the deep and diverse enduring effects of language on identity, stigma and belonging, showing how historical and modern terminology can shape children's and young people's lives. The language used in policies, legislation and professional practices parallels societal attitudes and impacts on how individuals view their own identity.

As we reconsider the frameworks, laws and policies which flavour our practice, it becomes clear that we must actively address language which harms. By embracing healing language, we can weave belonging in spaces where children feel accepted. This calls for a cultural shift within the professions that interact with children and young people. We must sustain our efforts for our practice to evolve and appreciate that working on language will require sustained attention.

Ultimately, a commitment to self awareness, ongoing learning and compassionate practice will lead to more inclusive and supportive services. As we strive to learn and improve, we must remember the profound impact our words can have. By choosing language that affirms and nurtures, we can help build a future where every child and young person truly feels they belong.

Key Chapter Takeaways

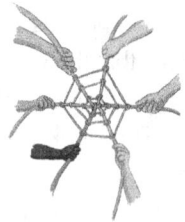

- Language can shape the identities and experiences of children and young people. The words we use, the words in policy and the words in everyday practice can either harm or heal, influencing how individuals perceive themselves and their place in society as children but also as the adults that they will become.
- The legacy of harmful terminology, such as 'maladjusted' or 'waifs and strays', lingers in modern practice, showing up as stigmatisation and othering.
- Bear in mind the importance of incorporating the concept of belonging in policy and legislation. While there are some emerging signs of this shift, such as the inclusion of

belonging in certain international policies and local strategies, there is still room for further work.
- By consciously choosing words that do not pathologise or marginalise children, together we can dismantle the stigma associated with being in care or excluded from school.

Reflection

How does my own use of language contribute to the identity and sense of belonging of the children and young people I work with? Is there anything that might unintentionally contribute to stigma or unbelonging?

In what ways can I actively contribute to the cultural shift needed in my profession to move from language that harms to language that heals?

How can I incorporate trauma-informed practices into my work, especially in terms of the language I use? How might this influence how I document and discuss the children and young people in my care?

References and Bibliography

Bristol City Council. (2021). *Bristol Belonging Strategy: Belonging from the Beginning 2021–2024*. Retrieved on 3 July 2023, from https://www.bristolonecity.com/wp-content/uploads/2021/10/2-Belonging-Strategy-Belonging-from-the-Beginning_weba_v2.pdf

Cherry, L. (2022). *The Brightness of Stars; Stories from Care Experienced Adults to Inspire Change* (3rd ed.). Abingdon: Routledge.

Coram Voice. (2020). Bright Spots insight paper on stigma. Retrieved on 19 June 2023 from https://coramvoice.org.uk/wp-content/uploads/2020/03/Bright-Spots-Insight-Paper-Stigma- web.pdf

Department for Education (DfE). (2023a). *Children's Social Care Reform.* Retrieved on 26 July 2024 from https://www.gov.uk/government/publications/childrens-social-care-reform-statement/childrens-social-care-reform-statement

Department for Education (DfE). (2023b). *Children's Social Care: Stable Homes, Built* on *Love Consultation Response.* Retrieved on 26 July 2024 from https://www.gov.uk/government/consultations/childrens-social-care-stable-homes-built-on-love

Dorset Council. (2023). *Dorset Strategic Alliance for Children and Young People.* Retrieved on 3 July 2023 from https://www.dorsetcouncil.gov.uk/-/children-young-people-and-families-plan-2023-to- 33

Fieller, D., & Loughlin, M. (2022). Stigma, epistemic injustice, and "looked after children": the need for a new language. *Journal of Evaluation in Clinical Practice*, 28(5): 867–874.

Haines, S. K.. (2019). *The Politics of Trauma.* North Atlantic Books.

Makovichuk, L., Hewes, J., Lirette, P., & Thomas, N. (2014). Play, participation, and possibilities: an early learning and child care curriculum framework for Alberta. Retrieved on 10 January 2023 from www.childcareframework.com

Manago, B., Davis, J. L., & Goar, C. (2022). The Stigma Discourse-Value Framework. *Comparative Sociology,* 21(3): 275–299.

National Society for the Prevention of Cruelty to Children (NSPCC). (2023). Why language matters: why you should avoid the acronym 'LAC' when talking about children in care. Retrieved on 21 November 2023 from https://learning.nspcc.org.uk/news/why-language-matters/looked-after-children

Roberts, L. M., & Dutton, J. E. (2009). *Exploring Positive Identities and Organizations: Building a Theoretical and Research Foundation.* Abingdon: Routledge.

Scottish Government. (2020). *The Promise Scotland.* Retrieved on 9 May 2023 from https://thepromise.scot/what-is-the-promise/about

The Adolescent and Children's Trust (TACT). (2019). Language that cares. Retrieved on 19 June 2023 from https://www.tactcare.org.uk/content/uploads/2019/03/TACT-Language-that-cares- 2019_online.pdf

The Early Years Learning Framework for Australia. (2022). Belonging, being and becoming. Retrieved on 26 July 2024 from https://www.acecqa.gov.au /sites/default/files/2023-01/EYLF-2022-V2.0.pdf

Tyler, I. (2020). *Stigma: The Machinery of Inequality* (1st ed.). London: Bloomsbury Publishing.

Williams, S. (2018). *Unmarried Motherhood in the Metropolis, 1700–1850: Pregnancy, the Poor Law and Provision* (1st ed.). Cham, Switzerland: Springer International Publishing.

6
Leadership is a Verb

Introduction

The importance of language has been explored in Chapter 5 and in continuing that thread, we can approach the word 'leadership' by understanding that it is much more than a word, and far more than a job title. You may be questioning where a chapter on leadership fits into a book about children and young people on belonging. In this chapter, we harness the idea that leadership is the responsibility of us all if we are to provide the level of belonging that every young person deserves.

DOI: 10.4324/9781003426592-9

Being a Leader is more than a Job Title

When leaders go on a transformative journey, they start to create magic for the children and young people who occupy all of the spaces they work in. Being a leader is not a job title; it is a decision. It is a decision that we can all make, we can choose to be a leader of hope. Transformational leadership in particular can enable teams of professionals to become a strong force as together, when we share a vision, we can achieve so much more for children and young people. We will consider how we can build a purposeful team around a child or young person through fostering spaces, places and services which utilise the full capabilities of every individual in the team.

My aim here is to further your thinking about how we establish an environment which will increase the child or young person's feeling of belonging through trust, collaboration and an inherent understanding that we all have an opportunity to flourish as growth after challenge can and does happen. Trauma-informed leadership means together we can be a powerful force to uplift our colleagues as well as the children and young people we support, and there is always hope. When each of us takes ownership and acts as a leader in our own way, we can role model this to others. In turn, we can celebrate the growth and development of the individuals which make up the whole. For this reason, the chapter will be leaning heavily on the Substance Abuse and Mental Health Services Administration's (SAMHSA's) six guiding principles of trauma-informed practice.

By continuing our weaving and drawing on these principles, we can create a rich blanket of support and compassion to wrap around the shoulders of the children and young people who were excluded and isolated on a number of levels. In doing so, we weave the most invaluable environments. Environments which cultivate healing and resilience. Environments which grow adults who will hopefully look back on their childhood experiences and be able to identify that they were valued, that they were heard and held. That they were nurtured in inclusive and nurturing cultures by adult leaders who made a difference ... for whom belonging didn't remain a dream, but became a reality.

Through trauma-informed leadership, we can also protect our most crucial resource ... the people in our spaces. The people who work in the spaces, places and services that work with children and young people. Koloroutis and Pole (2021) identified that when leaders embody trauma-informed practice, they are much more compassionate and understanding towards the challenges and experiences their colleagues may have and, in turn, have a greater emotional capacity to fully support the children and young people themselves. This might go some way to explaining why Alisha chose to use her social work qualification to work in adult services rather than children's services. After all, if we don't care for ourselves as adults, especially given the tough yet rewarding work we do, how can we nurture children and young people?

Fink-Samnick (2022) also reflects on how the environments we weave together can lead to support networks which increase our bandwidth to process the experiences of others. Thus we protect the mental health and wellbeing of ourselves and those around us. Investing in our own self-care is crucial in order to decrease the likelihood of stress and anxiety weaving a toxic, unhealthy web which contributes to burnout. This is why we all need to be leaders. We need to be able to step up when we see a colleague struggling. We need to be brave and courageous enough to identify and support others as well as recognise the signs in ourselves. This is why leaders are role models. You can be a role model irrespective of where you sit in the organisational hierarchy.

When cultivating safe, compassionate, trauma-informed spaces, consistency matters in order to maintain working environments which emphasise the importance of promoting staff wellbeing. Esaki et al. (2022) found that this can increase staff loyalty as they will feel more valued and supported. When we feel safe to be ourselves, we are more likely to think in more abstract ways, and work outside our comfort zones to our full potential (Batool et al., 2022). Now, this isn't to say that trauma-informed leaders won't sometimes encounter choppy waters, particularly amidst seas of change but leaders who understand on a profound level the needs of their teams can support them by resolving conflicts in a manner which dares to delve into the underlying issues that fuel the situation. Leaders who utilise such an approach are often viewed as being more understanding of the needs of others. Typically, this helps bonding and to knit teams more closely which in turn ripples down to the children and young people. After all, if we seek to seamlessly weave belonging, compassion and co-production throughout our environments, we can only do this by understanding trauma as well as what makes people tick. How we recognise, respond and relate to adults and children is fundamental to everyone, not just those who have an experience of trauma (Waller, 2020).

Creating Meaningful Connections

Having relationships that sit at the core of a non-hierarchical organisation really can be magic. But how can we achieve this in practice?

Thinking back to Chapter 4 where we explored the power of language, it is integral to leadership too! Language can revolutionise relationships in a myriad of ways. I have listed some suggested phrases in Figure 6.2 that will hopefully support your reflection on how we use language to get things done in the workplace.

What do you notice from these examples? Hopefully, you can see the focus is on learning together, on weaving shared values, collective interests and transparent communication through all we do. If we go right back to basics here, integrity, humility and honesty must be completely embodied. This isn't to say that being a leader is easy. There is a tremendous amount of responsibility we carry, and sometimes when we are time pressured or feeling burnt out ourselves, we can unintentionally make promises just to keep the peace. However, whilst this is often much quicker and can get us out of some sticky situations in the first instance, not over-promising and taking time to consider the full

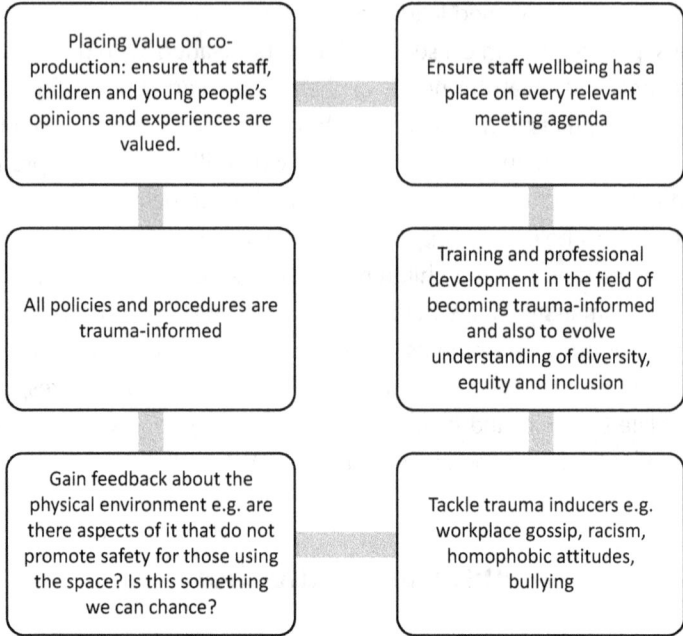

Figure 6.1 Making Connections in Trauma-Informed Leadership

situation will reap dividends and cut our workload in the long run. This is how the foundations of trust are built as sometimes being quick to act can unintentionally lead to team members feeling unvalued; this is particularly the case when we have to go back on our word at a later date.

When we make shared leadership our goal, undervalued and dissatisfied teams become a thing of the past. Motivating those around us to use their own life experience and wisdom can support the collective finding of innovative strategies as well promoting effective communication strategies to share common values. Through mechanisms such as these, it is also possible for leaders to demonstrate that they are consistent. Consistency is one way in which trust can be built with all team members knowing that they will be non-judgmentally listened

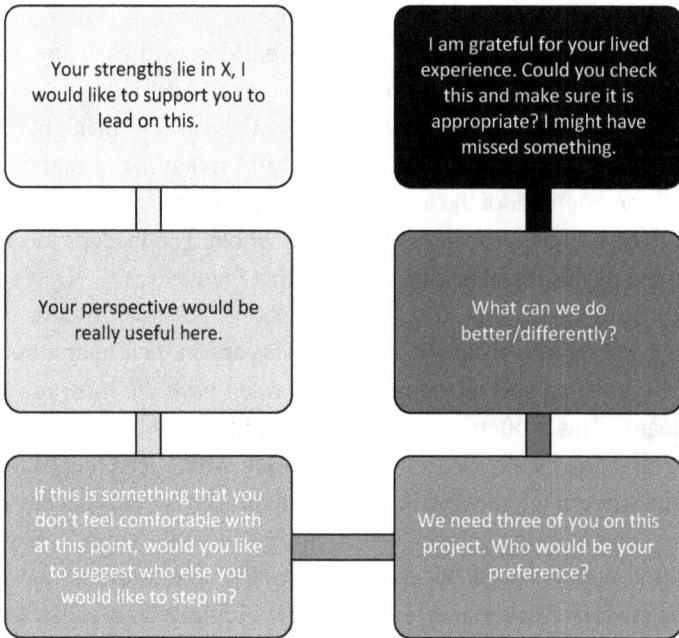

Figure 6.2 Developing Connections in Trauma-informed Leadership

to. This also makes it possible to be entirely equitable and for team members to understand that some individuals may require adaptations due to their circumstances in order to be treated fairly. For example, a colleague who has care responsibilities for an elderly relative may be granted the right to flexible hours. Equity doesn't mean treating everyone the same. Leaders that can make these decisions and justify them whilst ensuring they have considered all possibilities become trusted leaders. Leaders sometimes have to make difficult decisions where the outcomes may not be favourable, but when we see a leader who is taking on board the team's views and who wants to learn from those around them, this is more likely to be interpreted as a leader who can consider the best way forward in everyone's best interests. Gunnarsdóttir and Jónsdóttir (2013) recognise as the efforts of those who make an effort to foster relationships as being the mark of the leader who understands they need the backing of their team. They may have a different skill set from other people just like every other member of their team, but they are no greater or lesser than anybody else in the organisation. We may think of it much like a patchwork quilt. Every member of the team has their own square of fabric offering something unique and different from the whole. The leader's job is to stitch the pieces together and celebrate that uniqueness.

Morrison-Smith and Ruiz (2020) demonstrate that leaders who understand the drivers and barriers of everyone in their team through actively listening and relational working often have the most productive teams. This is often due to the increased sense of both feeling and being psychologically safe in the workplace which encourages open channels of communication for contributions. These approaches can further lead to a decrease in feeling the need to adorn ourselves with virtual armour or mask for fear of not being able to show our true selves at work (Tucker and Hoying, 2023). Adults who are able to be authentic can provide a much richer supportive experience for the children and young people they work with. They can only do this if their leader makes it feel safe to do so.

Emotional Intelligence

Just because we have the word 'leadership' or 'leader' in our title, there is no expectation for us to be a 'superhero', a flawless force that never makes mistakes. None of us like the thought of being viewed as weak and this can put pressure on us to be viewed as omniscient but, in reality, this typically has the opposite effect. Mistakes, naturally, can make us feel awkward and so the easiest thing to do in such a situation is to cover it up. Equally with difficult situations, we may take on the role of a protector and not share the full picture with our teams. However, just as wind whipping up the waves and pounding the water against a cliff will cause erosion over time, so covering up our mistakes or sugar coating a situation and the implications this has will lead to a breakdown of trust. Accepting our mistakes and owning our areas for improvement is exactly what we want to role model to our teams. What better way than this to role model our own integrity and to practise displaying acceptance? It certainly isn't always easy and will require a lot of bravery on the part of the leader but valuable lessons will be learnt by all. This is much better than the feelings of deception or betrayal when information gets leaked to the team or someone finds out the reality of the situation. Such situations can lead to a decrease in staff's confidence in their leader's abilities. Once relationships in the workplace are compromised, it takes a lot of work to rebuild them.

Being aware of and owning our mistakes as well as processing our own feelings around them are defined by Goleman (2006) as the signs of an emotionally intelligent individual. This quality refers to our ability to self-regulate and is seen as a critical component in creating lasting relationships. When we can balance compassion for others with sustaining our own boundaries, we will be rewarded by greater respect from our teams, as well as possess even greater resilience during trying times in the future. Goleman (2006) identifies the key ingredients required for emotional intelligence. First, self-awareness fuels our own personal reflections with regard to our strengths and areas for improvement. Understanding and working on this can enable us to create stronger and more cohesive teams. Furthermore, self regulation is paramount in order to address our own emotions and know when we need to ask for support or take some time out before addressing a difficulty with a member of the team. Social awareness and relationship management go hand in hand, and provide the tools to nurture others in a value-driven and solution-focused manner where everyone's strengths are brought to the fore. However, we can only promote belonging and lead our team in a psychologically safe manner if we also possess Goleman's final ingredient for motivation. When we have the determination, enthusiasm and energy to conduct transformational organisational change, we will be rewarded with a loyal team who have aspirations to improve the experience of young people using the space or service.

A practical idea to support being an emotionally intelligent individual would be to arrange team drop ins where everyone has a chance for their voice to be heard and valued. Additionally, a mentoring system could be created where staff support each other to address whatever problem presents itself. Ultimately, empathetic leaders are able to use discussion to avoid the hassle of misinterpreting a situation. A leader with empathy will ask thoughtful and meaningful questions and avoid making assumptions. To quote Steven Covey (2004, p. 235), 'Seek first to understand, then to be understood'.

Summary

Leadership is not confined to job titles; it is a collective responsibility where everyone can choose to lead, especially in fostering environments that promote trust, collaboration and growth. With a focus on transformational leadership, hopefully we now see the potential for positive change when we share a vision and empower our teams. Trauma-informed leadership, based on SAMHSA's principles, fosters resilience and supports both colleagues and the children they serve. These principles can be woven into the nurturing environments we seek to create in order to help children feel valued, heard and included, promoting their healing and resilience. And, if that isn't enough, leaders who embody trauma-informed practices can also support their colleagues' wellbeing, reducing stress and burnout, which enhances the collective capacity to care for the children and young people who rely on these leaders and their staff. Finally, emotionally intelligent leaders who are self-aware, empathetic and capable of managing relationships can build trust, promote psychological safety and lead teams effectively through challenging situations.

Key Chapter Takeaways

- Leadership is an active, transformative process that anyone can undertake. Being a leader is about making decisions and taking actions that inspire those around us.
- Leadership is crucial in creating environments where children and young people feel they belong. Transformative leadership can have a significant impact on the spaces utilised by children and young people, and enables us to weave opportunities for belonging throughout spaces.
- When we focus on fostering connections within our teams and consider everything through a trauma-informed lens, we are more likely to retain motivated, happy and healthy staff.
- Fostering transparent and open communication builds trust, especially when we consider our language choices.

Reflection

How can I work towards sharing the organisational vision with my team in a way that values everyone's input?

How could SAMHSA's values support me in my role?

What aspects of my own self-care could I review and how could I role model self-care to the team? Are there aspects of Goleman's Emotional Intelligence Ingredients I would like to improve further?

References and Bibliography

Batool, F., Mohammad, J., & Awang, S. R. (2022). The effect of servant leadership on organisational sustainability: the parallel mediation role of creativity and psychological resilience. *Leadership & Organization Development Journal,* 43 (1): 71–95. https://doi.org/10.1108/LODJ-06-2021-0264

Covey, S. R. (2004). *The 7 Habits of Highly Effective People: Restoring the Character Ethic.* New York, NY: Simon & Schuster.

Esaki, N., Reddy, M., & Bishop, C. T. (2022). Next steps: applying a trauma-informed model to create an anti-racist organizational culture. *Behavioral Sciences* (Basel, Switzerland), 12(2): 41. https://doi.org/10.3390/bs12020041

Fink-Samnick, E. (2022). Collective occupational trauma, health care quality, and trauma-informed leadership: intersections and implications. *Professional Case Management,* 27(3): 107–123. https://doi.org/10.1097/NCM.0000000000000559

Goleman, D. (2006). *Emotional Intelligence* (10th anniversary ed.). New York: Bantam Books.

Gunnarsdóttir, S., & Birna Jónsdóttir, G. (2013). Servant leadership and research in Iceland. *Stjórnmál Og Stjórnsýsla,* 9(2): 415–438. https://doi.org/10.13177/irpa.a.2013.9.2.8

Koloroutis, M., & Pole, M. (2021). Trauma-informed leadership and posttraumatic growth. *Nursing Management,* 52(12): 28–34. https://doi.org/10.1097/01.NUMA.0000800336.39811.a3

Morrison-Smith, S., & Ruiz, J. (2020). Challenges and barriers in virtual teams: a literature review. *SN Applied Sciences,* 2(6): 1096–.

Tucker, S., & Hoying, J. (2023). Empathic communication Part I: responding to stress in the workplace. In J. E. Davidson & , M. Richardson (Eds.), *Workplace Wellness: From Resiliency to Suicide Prevention and Grief Management.* Cham, Switzerland: Springer. https://doi.org/10.1007/978-3-031-16983-0_11

Waller, L. (2020). Fostering a sense of belonging in the workplace: enhancing well-being and a positive and coherent sense of self. In S. Dhiman (Ed.), *The Palgrave Handbook of Workplace Well-being,* 1–27.

7

Intersection and Intersectionality

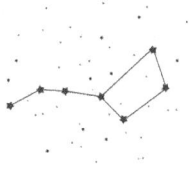

Introduction

In this chapter, I explore intersections and intersectionality as important considerations within the work of trauma-informed practice and cultivating belonging. I go on to contest the tendency I've observed in how we work with children and young people, in research and in policy, which is the reduction of a person's identity to a single aspect of their living experience, for example, being a child in care or a child with SEND. However, I do this with some caution as I also acknowledge that defining one experience over others can be incredibly influential across a person's life. Our childhood experiences define us as we develop and grow, and our brain's architecture wires up according to the particular contexts that we find ourselves in. But we also live beyond these formative experiences. Unpacking our childhood in adulthood, making conscious the taken for granted, discarding and keeping what we choose may be likened to an old suitcase full of clothes opened at various points throughout life where we keep some of them and discard others. The paradox of defining but not being defined by is rarely explored as care-experienced adults of all ages are seldom asked to explore it. There is little dialogue or research that explores how political, cultural and social forces shape adults *after* care (Hugman et al., 2016). This chapter invites us all to think about and consider our positionality which speaks to our multiple identities and how they are experienced by us.

'Intersectionality' and 'intersection' have distinct meanings in sociology and social justice and it feels prudent to make this distinction known.

Care as a Defining Experience

Living within the care system is not a mainstream experience; about 1 per cent of children, at any one time, are looked after away from home formally (there are informal arrangements that will not be recorded by the Department of Education's annual collection from local authorities). About 3 per cent of children are in receipt of services and support from children's social care at any one time (Ofsted, 2020). Furthermore, one study looking at a child's first entry into care found that 1 in 30 children in England will experience at least one episode of being in care before their 18th birthday (McGrath-Lone et al., 2016).

The research exposes the reality of the multiple adversities experienced through living in care, through being separated from family relationships and communities and recovering from the loss of education. The fight for survival is present in the data in various ways. For the research, I gathered wisdom through a survey, one-to-one interviews and a biographical writing task. It was in this writing task that I found depth and richness. I simply asked people to write in no more than 250 words what belonging meant for them. The first verse of a poem written for the biographical writing task talked about fighting, but with a sense of resistance to it, as though the writer really had no option but to fight.

Table 7.1 Intersectionality and Intersection

Intersectionality	Intersectionality is a sociological framework developed by Kimberlé Crenshaw in 1989, which sought to address the impact of being a woman of colour and how those identities intersected to create unique experiences of discrimination and privilege. Crenshaw introduced this concept to highlight the compounded nature of oppression which could not be understood through the singular category of identity alone. Intersectionality posits that different forms of discrimination (e.g., racism, sexism) do not operate independently but are interconnected, creating complex layers of disadvantage. Everyone's experience is shaped by the intersection of their various identities.
Intersection	Intersection refers to the overlapping or converging of multiple social identities within an individual. These identities can include aspects such as gender, race, ethnicity, class, sexual orientation, religion and disability and, in the case of this book, being in care and excluded from school. Intersection focuses on individual identity components, emphasising the multi-layered nature of personal identity. There is a recognition that different aspects of identity influence one another.

Positionality

In Chapter 1, I introduced the concept of positionality and shared mine with you. It is in paying close attention to positionality that the issue of cultural humility becomes centralised. The understanding that we have not lived another person's life and therefore cannot understand it without curiosity and humility (Abe, 2020) is embedded in this book, in my work and in the research that underpins this book. However, openness, self-awareness and egolessness are attributed to cultural humility in practice (Foronda et al., 2016) and the discussion about whether we can truly be 'egoless' is too broad to tackle here.

Cultural humility focuses on placing lived experiences at the centre of service/education delivery that reduces stigmatisation, marginalisation and further traumatisation within service/education provision. Research findings consistently suggest that compared to those that aren't, children in care are at an increased risk of adverse life outcomes such as mental ill health (Seker et al., 2022), social marginalisation (Social Market Foundation, 2018) and contact with the criminal justice system (Howard League, 2018; ONS, 2022). Internationally, children and young people in care show the same educational challenges and comparable outcomes. These include a lower average educational performance than their peers (DfE, 2022). Additionally, research suggests a strong association between educational outcomes and life outcomes.

Additional Needs

A high proportion of children in care have been observed as having accessed special educational needs (SEN) provision. A recent study found that of the 6,240 school-aged children who entered the care system, 83 per cent received provision for SEN at some point during those school years (Jay and Gilbert, 2021). This creates a picture of vulnerability for those who were in care as children and an even further layer of vulnerability across the life course for those who were also excluded from school. An important consideration here is that many children with special educational needs and disabilities (SEND) needs are likely to be related to adverse experiences before or during care so they are more likely to be SEMH issues. It may also be that some SEND increase the pressure in the family and may lead to an increase in the chance of being brought into care. A recent research project investigated the educational trajectories of children in care who entered school in 2005 and who took their GCSEs in 2016. One of the findings of this longitudinal study suggested that broader forms of disadvantage such as gender, ethnicity, socio-economic status and SEND had more to do with educational attainment than care itself (Berridge et al., 2020). That said, the exploration of child welfare and education in policy in Chapter 3 and this chapter's review of the academic literature highlight that the experiences of a child in care are likely to intersect with other experiences of marginalisation and can therefore lead to disadvantage. The Timpson Review (2019) reports that there is a trend for children who have received support from social care to be excluded from school, both through fixed-term exclusions and permanent exclusions. This group of children includes any child with a social worker, so not necessarily a child in care. For example, this would include children in need (CIN) of help or protection, including children in care, previously looked-after children (adopted children) and children under Special Guardianship or Child Arrangement Orders. Timpson goes on to report that being in need of help and protection has an association with poor educational outcomes. However, prior to the time that we collected national data on children in care and their educational attainment, Brodie (2000) examined the evidence regarding school exclusion with a particular focus on children who were living in residential care placements. At that time, Brodie argues, much more was known about the educational experiences of children living in residential accommodation than about those in foster care. Brodie's research suggests that alternative views on exclusion are required with regard to children who are in care. These are exclusion by non-admission, exclusion upon admission, graduated exclusion or progressive isolation, planned exclusion and, finally, exclusion from school and professional intervention. Brodie (2000) suggested, over 23 years ago, that more research into this intersection of care and exclusion was required.

The research available regarding poorer outcomes for those who were excluded from school (Welsh and Little, 2018; DfE, 2019) indicates a need to further study the impact of exclusion on those who were excluded from school and were also children in care. The various intersections experienced by children in care are further compounded by the multiple intersections experienced by those children excluded from school. Additionally, marginalised groups have intersected and continue to intersect with exclusion and therefore with further marginalisation, inequalities and inequity in their adult lives (Thompson and Menter, 2017; Thompson et al., 2021). Research has consistently shown that children classified as having SEND are more likely to experience layers of disadvantage such as living in rented accommodation, in single parent households and in poverty (Daniels et al., 2019).

Mental Health, SEND and Wellbeing

Children and young people with mental health challenges are more likely to be excluded from school (Fazel and Newby, 2021). Black Caribbean pupils have been shown to be four times more likely to be excluded from school than the rest of the school population (Demie, 2021) and a child with learning difficulties is nine times more likely to be permanently excluded (O'Brien and Gilbert, 2016). Martin-Denham (2021) argues that inadequate SEND support in schools accounts for the prevalence of exclusion rates for children with SEND. Children with identified SEND are entitled to receive support in school but where that is deemed inadequate, an Education, Health and Care Plan (EHCP) will be applied for. However, a recent report found SEND identification is variable depending on the school and area. There is a mismatch between how schools and local authorities identify children with SEND, and children who have suffered abuse or neglect have a reduced chance of being identified as having SEND (Nuffield Foundation and EPI, 2021). The report found that it was not until after a full year in care that the chances of being identified with SEND were greater than those of other children (Nuffield Foundation and EPI, 2021, p. 8).

As of January 2024, there were 576,000 children and young people with an EHCP, a number which has increased each year since 2010 (DfE, 2021). Children who are adopted, a subgroup of previously looked after children, were found to be 20 times more likely to be excluded from school, and over half of the children who were represented in this study had recognised SEND (Adoption UK, 2017). The same report found that a quarter of the children who were excluded had a somewhat questionable informal exclusion, suggesting a deeper look is required into how we think of the term 'school exclusion'.

Naming Exclusion

Illegal exclusions take many forms. Hidden from the data is off-rolling, the practice of removing a pupil from the school roll yet not formally excluding that pupil (Power and Taylor, 2020). Often the parents are then forced to home educate without any resources or support for the young person. There are also what are termed 'managed moves', this refers to moves arranged after a discussion between those involved in the education of the child from one school to another avoiding the need to exclude (Done and Knowler, 2020). Social, cultural and structural factors, such as apportioning blame to children and young people in the name of behaviourist approaches in schools, the presence of racism, classism and sexism and a failure to understand aspiration as hopes and dreams, are embedded in the system. These aspects appear to ensure that children and young people who already face disadvantages are destined to face even more (Gillies, 2016). Further evidence in support of the view that the system itself is simply not designed for children who are already marginalised can be found in exploring mental health and school (Robertson, 2021), children with a social worker and school (Millard, 2021) and geographically based inequalities between schools (Baars, 2021).

Drawing on Bronfenbrenner's Theory of Ecology, Bourdieu's Theory of Social and Cultural Capital and the Theory of Intersectionality, Welsh and Little's (2018) comprehensive literature review explores the connection between school exclusion and outcomes. This includes looking at pupil achievement, test scores, graduation rates, belongingness in school and contact with the Youth Justice System. Their review suggests exclusion impacts a range of academic outcomes, a strong correlation between exclusion and contact with the Youth Justice System and an association with a host of adverse life outcomes. In conclusion, they note the effects of exclusion are under-theorised, but have significant education policy and equity implications (Welsh and Little, 2018).

In a longitudinal study focusing on the impact of exclusion on employment, Madia et al. (2022) used data from the 'Next Steps' study, revisiting young people up to the age of 25/26 who had experienced school exclusion in early adolescence. The study found that there was a correlation between school exclusion and an increased risk of being unemployed, of being economically inactive and earning less. They also concluded that school exclusion does in fact represent a precursor to exclusion from society in adulthood. As such, they suggest the implications of exclusion should be understood as including the impact on the individual, and also that the wider society should be better informed about the costs of excluding children and young people from school as little is known about this (Madia et al., 2022). School exclusion was found to show short- and long-term difficulties, both in terms of psychological implications and life outcomes including a connection between exclusion and knife carrying and drug use (Martin-Denham, 2020). There is also some evidence that children who were excluded from school can experience high levels of psychological distress in comparison to their peers (Ford et al., 2021). While this research shows a correlation between school exclusion and poor outcomes, a causal connection was not confirmed.

The literature demonstrates how researchers have grappled with the complex interplay of a multitude of intersections, although perspectives from those who have lived through these experiences as children have too often been ignored. Introducing intersectionality as an analytical tool that facilitates understanding of care and exclusion increases the experience of these areas as marginalising. Intersectionality is rooted in black feminist and critical race theory and offers a way to move away from marginalisation and exclusion, and into thinking about social empowerment and reconstruction (Crenshaw, 1991). Furthermore, the concept of intersectionality provides a tool to understand social inequality and inequity, and enables us to think beyond one-dimensional explanations for marginalisation, stigmatisation and inequity (Hill Collins, 2016). As a theory, it helps us think through how different aspects of ourselves in the society in which we live and the time that we are born influence and interplay with each other.

Let's Take A Moment …

We're about to explore the impact and trauma of racism. It's time for some grounding either before or after you read the next section. You choose.

Music is very grounding, healing and a medium by which many of us express our internal emotional words. Here are a few suggestions on using music to ground yourself:

What was the last music that you danced to? Play it now and dance! Can't remember? Find something you love and dance.

Create a playlist that is specifically for listening to when you need to ground yourself.

As you listen to your playlist, doodle or draw and notice the images, the colours and the words you use.

Racism

The literature review undertaken in the research informs the view that we have a powerful human need, a motivation, to belong, and pursuing this need and motivation involves a dynamic process. From this starting point, the wisdom gathered highlights that how we feel about ourselves is informed by how we interact with the relationships available to us (the FACES), the environments or settings we find ourselves in (SPACES) and the community contexts we are engaged in (PLACES). Of the latter two terms: "place is bounded and specific ... space [is] more abstract, unlimited" (Gieseking and Mangold, 2014, p. xix). In this dynamic experience, how we feel about ourselves in relation to belonging changes depending on those FACES, SPACES and PLACES. The complexity of this need to belong, in parallel with whether it is believed that belonging is deserved, alongside access to relationships (faces) and settings (SPACES) and community localities (PLACES), explains why some of the participants talk about it taking years to find a sense of belonging. Furthermore, the tenacity demonstrated in trying to belong is profound. This is particularly prevalent in the case of participants who experienced racism, either directly or in the context of the anticipation of racism.

For Jenny felt that by changing her name, she may be more accepted:

> I actually changed my name by deed poll for a more white sounding name because they would you know my Indian name.
>
> (Jenny)

Jenny also shares her concerns about being the only 'non-white' child in her school, highlighting the words 'segregation', 'terrorism' and 'racial tensions':

> The big one for me and schooling was that I went to quite an affluent school in the area, and it was a CofE school. And I was the only non-white person there and in the area that without saying the name, there was lots of racial tensions, there was the terrorist attacks that were happening and the community itself was very segregated.
>
> (Jenny)

James too spent a lot of time reflecting on his own race, questioning his sense of belonging:

> As a black boy (mixed race – increasing my sense of not being one or another) I didn't feel I belonged where I found myself – A children's home in a new town on the outskirts of London. I got into lots of fights at school as I was one of very few people of colour in the town.
>
> (James)

Finally, Sam also felt a need to try to change his outward appearance in the hope that he would gain increased acceptance:

> I was bullied for being mixed race after I moved to a predominantly white area council estate. I would explore any way I could to become 'white' like them, I put talc on my face, hated my dad for being Indian, tried to dress like my peers but couldn't always afford it.
>
> (Sam)

The quotes above demonstrate how the intersectionality between being in care and being excluded from school was experienced through the lived experience of being 'black' or 'mixed race' or 'non-white' in the United Kingdom across a variety of decades. The participants span different decades, conjuring up different cultural references that would have resided neatly within the environmental fabric of those living through it. Each decade provides a backdrop with regard to that intersection of experience. For example, the 1960s saw Conservative MP, Enoch Powell during the first reading of the Race Relations Bill make his infamous Rivers of Blood Speech (Powell, 1968) where he deplored the fact that 'In this country in 15 or 20 years' time the black man will have the whip hand over the white man.' The 1970s saw the National Front, a far-right political party which had formed in

1967 using immigration as its central issue, peak and win 18.3 per cent of the vote in Leicester (McCarthy, 2021). In the early 1980s, of Lord Scarman's report in which he was asked to conduct an inquiry into what were termed the Brixton Riots sparked by tensions between the police and the black community with violent assaults on those of South Asian descent was released. That period also saw uprisings or riots breaking out across the United Kingdom where there were substantial black community populations. In 1993, Stephen Lawrence was brutally murdered in Eltham, London, in a racially motivated attack leading to decades of holding the police to account for their failure to ensure that the murderers were convicted. The noughties commenced with the racially motivated murder of Damilola Taylor who was a 10-year-old Nigerian boy, with the police, yet again, being accused of a lack of progress in bringing the perpetrators to justice. The participants were all children and/or young people during his period and consequently it is not surprising that the experience of racism played such a large part in searching for belonging as a child in care, and also as a child excluded from school. The data show that in searching for belonging, the participants had employed a range of strategies to manage exclusion, whether that was from home, from school, from country or from culture.

> The main thing was that I would do absolutely ANYTHING to fit in. This included sleeping around at a very early age, running away from home and becoming a Tomboy.
>
> (Sam)

Thus, searching for belonging may have involved FACES, SPACES and PLACES that were harmful. In fact, belonging was found to be the most important criteria for participants, regardless of whether the context for that belonging was good for a person or not. This finding is consistent with research around motivations for joining gangs. Belonging can be fulfilled through connectedness with others, which also then validates one's social identity (Bolger and Needs, 2022).

> Glue sniffing was my escape. I could forget all my loneliness and feelings high on glue. The funny thing is that I did feel a sense of belonging with the group of kids I hung about with. All came from broken homes where no one cared if they were out late graffitiing town and nicking cars. We looked after each other, protected each other and hunted together – hunted for trouble, any kind.
>
> (James)

It is worth noting how the pursuit of belonging, especially through those pursuits mentioned by James, are often the areas that are socially stigmatising. This in turn can create further stigmatisation and may result in having further contact with services in adulthood such as mental health services, drug and alcohol services and criminal justice services.

Endurance

It may well be the case that it is one's capacity for endurance of not just adversity but also of living with the impact of that adversity without relational wealth that supports overcoming it and becoming resilient. The word 'endurance' tends to feature more frequently when talking about the capacity of a sports person than the ability to live through adversity and trauma without sufficient relational networks. However endurance provides another way of thinking about why many people can grow and heal and find meaningful relationships and lives as adults when childhood was so harsh.

Some participants used the term 'resilience', and others described qualities that might be described as resilience. Notwithstanding the extensive research base on resilience and the overuse of it as a concept in relation to children particularly, the need to understand why some people can thrive after adversity and trauma in childhood will always remain of interest to those working with those children. The word 'resilience' can evoke negative reactions for people who have endured adversity and trauma as children. However this research suggests that it is plausible to think of resilience as having the ability to achieve in educational contexts, the capacity to engage in relationships should they be available and the ability to have the basic needs of housing, food and warmth met. These fundamental rights are the stepping stones towards resiliency but might also be considered as 'positive outcomes'. The research suggests that this is the view of the participants. However, there is also a view that resilience is 'coming through' something and being 'ok' afterwards.

Summary

What we can take from this chapter is that intersectionality recognises some of the many other areas that intersect with care and with exclusion such as race, gender, class, SEND, poverty, mental health and criminal justice. The inception of intersectionality as a critical theory invites the reader, the author, ordinary people, the policy maker and the practitioner to think differently about the problem (Hill Collins, 2016). A review of the literature highlights the complex ways in which people experience marginalisation across the multiple identities they have, and it is simply not possible to think about care, exclusion and belonging without also thinking about intersectionality.

This chapter has sought to demonstrate how drawing on Hill Collins' (2016) concept of intersectionality can strengthen an understanding of marginalisation, stigmatisation and inequity in relation to being in care. In doing so, I recommend those working with children in care and also those researching children in care should consider how being a child in care is a further dimension of intersectionality, and one which is often ignored in the literature. Furthermore, if the focus remains solely on an individual's identity as 'being a child in care', there is a risk of missing the complexity of how a person's experience is also impacted by other marginalising experiences. In other words, we are complex, we have multiple identities that are experienced culturally, socially and politically and no-one can be reduced to just one aspect of self.

Key Chapter Takeaways

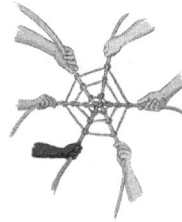

- Intersectionality is critical to minimise the likelihood of reducing a person's identity to a single aspect, such as being in care.
- While being care-experienced is certainly a powerful factor which can shape a person's life, it is not the only defining aspect. Individuals move beyond their childhood experiences, and it's essential to recognise the ongoing process of unpacking and integrating these experiences throughout life.
- When we acknowledge our own positionality we start to meaningfully comprehend and support diverse experiences whilst also demonstrating that we cannot know what we have not lived.
- Intersectionality aids our understanding of how overlapping disadvantages can impact educational and life outcomes. The search for belonging can sometimes lead to harmful behaviours and further marginalisation which demonstrates why we need to be designing the services, spaces and places that are utilised by all young people in a way that is truly supportive and inclusive.

Reflection

Are you aware of your positionality? How does it shape your practice?

How can you support care-experienced individuals in unpacking and integrating their childhood experiences as they grow older?

How can you ensure that the services, spaces, and places you design and work in are truly supportive and inclusive of diverse identities and experiences?

References and Bibliography

Abe, J. (2020). Beyond cultural competence, toward social transformation: liberation psychologies and the practice of cultural humility. *Journal of Social Work Education,* 56(4): 696–707.

Adoption UK. (2017). Adoption UK's schools & exclusions report. Retrieved on 23 July 2024 from https://production.basw.co.uk/sites/default/files/resources/basw_45038-5.pdf

Baars, S. (2021). Area-based inequalities and the new frontiers in education policy. In I. Menzies & S. Baars (Eds.), *Young People on the Margins: Priorities for Action in Education and Youth* (1st ed.). London: Routledge.

Berridge, D., Luke, N., Sebba, J., Strand, S., Cartwright, M., Staples, E. M., McGrath-Lone, L., Ward, J., & O'Higgins, A. (2020). Children in need and children in care: educational attainment and progress. Retrieved on 2 August 2024 from https://www.education.ox.ac.uk/wp-content/uploads/2020/06/Final-Report-Nuffield.pdf

Bolger, L., & Needs, A. (2022). An interpretative phenomenological analysis of the experience of ex-gang members as they transition into and out of gangs. *Journal of Forensic Psychology Research and Practice,* 22(2): 186–219.

Brady, E., & Gilligan, R. (2018). The life course perspective: an integrative research paradigm for examining the educational experiences of adult care leavers? *Children and Youth Services Review*, 87: 69–77.

Brodie, I. (2000). Children's homes and school exclusion: redefining the problem. *Support for Learning*, 15(1): 25–29.

Crenshaw, K. (1991). Mapping the margins: intersectionality, identity politics, and violence against women of color. *Stanford Law Review*, 43(6): 1241–1299.

Daniels, H., Thompson, I., & Tawell, A. (2019). Practices of exclusion in cultures of inclusive schooling in the United Kingdom. *Revista Publicaciones*, 49(3): 23–36.

Demie, F. (2021). The experience of black Caribbean pupils in school exclusion in England. *Educational Review* (Birmingham), 73(1): 55–70.

Department for Education (DfE). (2019). *School Exclusion: A Literature Review on the Continued Disproportionate Exclusion of Certain Children.* Retrieved on 2 August 2024 from https://assets.publishing.service.gov .uk/media/5cd15de640f0b63329d700e5/Timpson_review_of_school _exclusion_literature_review.pdf

Department for Education (DfE). (2021). *Children Looked After in England Including Adoptions.* Retrieved on 27 June 2022 from https://explore -education-statistics.service.gov.uk/find-statistics/children-looked-after-in -england-including-adoptions/2021

Department for Education (DfE). (2022). *Statutory Guidance. School Suspensions and Permanent Exclusions.* Retrieved on 9 May 2023 from https://www.gov.uk/government/publications/school-exclusion.

Done, E., & Knowler, H. (2020). Painful invisibilities: roll management or 'off-rolling' and professional identity. *British Educational Research Journal*, 46(3): 516–531.

Fazel, M., & Newby, D. (2021). Mental well-being and school exclusion: changing the discourse from vulnerability to acceptance. *Emotional and Behavioural Difficulties*, 26(1): 78–86.

Ford, T., Degli Esposti, M., Crane, C., Taylor, L., Montero-Marín, J., Blakemore, S.-J., Bowes, L., Byford, S., Dalgleish, T., Greenberg, M. T., Nuthall, E., Phillips, A., Raja, A., Ukoumunne, O. C., Viner, R. M., Williams, J. M. G., Allwood, M., Aukland, L., Casey, T., & Kuyken, W. (2021). The role of schools in early adolescents' mental health: findings from the MYRIAD Study. *Journal of the American Academy of Child and Adolescent Psychiatry*, 60(12): 1467–1478.

Foronda, C., Baptiste, D., Reinholdt, M. M., & Ousman, K. (2016). Cultural humility. *Journal of Transcultural Nursing*, 27(3), 210–217.

Gieseking, J. J., & Mangold, W. (Eds.). (2014). *The people, place, and space reader*. New York: Routledge.

Gillies, V. (2016). *Pushed to the Edge: Inclusion and Behaviour Support in Schools* (University Press Scholarship Online). Bristol: Policy Press.

Hill Collins, P., & Bilge, S. (2016). *Intersectionality*. Oxford: Polity Press.

Howard League. (2018). Ending the criminalisation of children in residential care. Retrieved on 2 August 2024 from https://howardleague.org/publications/ending-the-criminalisation-of-children-in-residential-care

Hugman, C., Harding, J., & Cieslik, M (2016). What's the story? Sociological explorations of the life course narratives of adults with care experience, PQDT – UK & Ireland.

Jay, M. A., & Gilbert, R. (2021). Special educational needs, social care and health. *Archives of Disease in Childhood*, 106(1), 83–85. https://doi.org/10.1136/archdischild-2019-317985

Madia, J. E., Obsuth, I., Thompson, I., Daniels, H., & Murray, A. L. (2022). Long-term labour market and economic consequences of school exclusions in England: evidence from two counterfactual approaches. *British Journal of Educational Psychology*, 92(3): 801–816.

Martin-Denham, S. (2020). Riding the rollercoaster of school exclusion coupled with drug misuse: the lived experience of caregivers. *Emotional and Behavioural Difficulties*, 25(3–4): 244–263.

Martin-Denham, S. (2021). Defining, identifying, and recognising underlying causes of social, emotional and mental health difficulties: thematic analysis of interviews with headteachers in England. *Emotional and Behavioural Difficulties*, 26(2): 187–205. https://doi.org/10.1080/13632752.2021.1930909

McCarthy, L. (2021). *The National Front and the BNP in Leicester and Leicestershire. University of Leicester*. Preprint.

McGrath-Lone, L., Dearden, L., Nasim, B., Harron, K., & Gilbert, R. (2016). Changes in first entry to out-of-home care from 1992 to 2012 among children in England. *Child Abuse & Neglect*, 51: 163–171.

Millard, W. (2021) Children who come into contact with social services. In L. Menzies & S. Baars (Eds.), *Young People on the Margins: Priorities for Action in Education and Youth* (1st ed.). London.

Nuffield Foundation, & Education Policy Institute (EPI). (2021). Identifying pupils with special educational needs and disabilities. Retrieved on 23

June 2021 from https://epi.org.uk/publications-and-research/identifying-send

O'Brien, J., & Gilbert, I. (2016). *Don't Send Him in Tomorrow: Shining a Light on the Marginalised, Disenfranchised and Forgotten Children of Today's Schools*. Bancyfelin: Crown House Publishing..

Office for National Statistics (ONS). (2022). The education background of looked-after children who interact with the criminal justice system. Retrieved in December 2024 from https://www.ons.gov.uk/peoplepopulationandcommunity/educationandchildcare/articles/thee   ducationbackgroundoflookedafterchildrenwhointeractwiththecriminaljusticesystem/december 2022

Ofsted, (2020). *Children's Social Care in England*. Retrieved on 2 August 2024 from https://www.gov.uk/government/statistics/childrens-social-care-data-in-england-2020/main-findings-childrens-social-care-in-england-2020#:~:text=Four%20in%20five%20homes%20(1%2C850,with%2018%25%20in%202019)

Powell, E. (1968) *Speech at Birmingham, 20 April*. Retrieved on 2 August 2024 from www.enochpowell.net/fr-79.html

Power, S., & Taylor, C. (2020). Not in the classroom, but still on the register: Hidden forms of school exclusion. *International Journal of Inclusive Education*, 24(8): 867–881.

Robertson, A. (2021) in Menzies, L., & Baars, S. (2021). *Young People on the Margins: Priorities for Action in Education and Youth* (1st ed.). London: Routledge.

Seker, S., Boonmann, C., Gerger, H., Jäggi, L., d'Huart, D., Schmeck, K., & Schmid, M. (2022). Mental disorders among adults formerly in out-of-home care: a systematic review and meta-analysis of longitudinal studies. *European Child & Adolescent Psychiatry*, 31(12): 1963–1982.

Social Market Foundation, (2018). Looked after children; the silent crisis. Retrieved on 23 March 2023 from https://www.smf.co.uk/wp-content/uploads/2018/08/Silent-Crisis-PDF.pdf

Thompson, I., & Menter, I. (2017). Tackling social disadvantage in the classroom. *In Tackling Social Disadvantage through Teacher Education*. St Albans: Critical Publishing.

Thompson, I., Tawell, A., & Daniels, H. (2021). Conflicts in professional concern and the exclusion of pupils with SEMH in England. *Emotional and Behavioural Difficulties,* 26(1): 31–45.

Timpson Review. (2019). School exclusion: a literature review on the continued disproportionate exclusion of certain children. Retrieved on 2 August 2024 from https://assets.publishing.service.gov.uk/government/uploads/system/uploads/attachment_data/file/807862/Timpson_review.pdf

Welsh, R. O., & Little, S. (2018). Caste and control in schools: a systematic review of the pathways, rates and correlates of exclusion due to school discipline. *Children and Youth Services Review,* 94: 315–339.

PART THREE:
Reconceptualising Weaving the Web: FACES, SPACES and PLACES

8
FACES That Make a Difference

Introduction

It was important to me to share with you the conceptual model of belonging that arose from the research. I also wanted a phrase that was easy to remember and easy to understand. Somewhat simplistically, I've settled on 'FACES, SPACES and PLACES', a direct interpretation of the findings of my research which was a model gifted by participants to assist the cultivation of belonging in any setting, service or system. But what does 'FACES, SPACES and PLACES' mean? In this chapter, I will describe 'FACES' and then in the following two chapters, I will in turn address 'SPACES' and 'PLACES'.

FACES

FACES refers not just to the relationships that we might think about when focusing on what relationships exist for the child, young person or family, but also extends to the FACES that make up whatever community we're thinking about. There are also the FACES that we see regularly and might say hello to but these might not be the FACES that provide relational depth. I live in a smallish market town. If I think about this community and the FACES as I walk through the town, there

DOI: 10.4324/9781003426592-12

are close friends that I might see, baristas in coffee shops who ask me if I'd like my usual and then people who spend their days walking up and down the street who I don't know but see regularly. All of these people give me a feeling of belonging in this town. It is worth adding that this is not the town of my childhood (of which there were many), nor where I lived for most of my adulthood. However, I have created enough connections for it to feel like my town, like a PLACE where I belong, is full of FACES that tell me that I belong here every day.

What might those FACES 'do' to help people develop a sense of belonging to a community?

How do FACES cultivate belonging?

Felt safety

Attunement

Connection

Empathic reassurance

Throughout this book, we have focused on relationships and explored the impact on people of not having meaningful, safe and longstanding relationships. The research discovered that the impact is profound. The idea of FACES reflects the pervasiveness of social encounters and the importance of meaningful relationships within them; FACES that tell us we are safe, FACES that we recognise, FACES that tell us we are in the right PLACE, FACES that mirror back to us that we belong. Relationship-focused practices in education and in children's social care make an important difference to those children and young people who need it the most and have far fewer high-quality relational opportunities to rely on. In other words, some of us need more FACES than others and we all need some FACES to stay the same; consistency matters. This is why it is so important that we offer a warm greeting to children and young people when we see them, that we think about our own facial expressions and how our FACE will be remembered by the young person. An experience which would have greatly benefited Maisie. As stated earlier, children in care have an ongoing merry-go-round of new FACES to navigate across various settings and from various services and systems.

> I couldn't cope, I just needed one warm person to be there and be consistent and that I could trust and depend on.
>
> (Maisie)

Not having a sense of belonging with anyone who looked after you when you are in care and also feeling as though the family you were born into is not where you belong is illuminated by Alisha who explores abandonment:

> There is a sense of people are abandoned if they don't belong somewhere. So when you don't belong you are abandoned and that's just kind of ....With belonging I've never, I don't, even now, as an adult, I don't feel I belong anywhere because I don't talk to .... I don't have secure foster carers, that I, you know, lived with, that I flourished with that I can say I oh, I belong in their family. Uhm, I definitely don't belong in my family, in fact my birth family is very dysfunctional.
>
> (Alisha)

It could be argued that this has led to many of us asking 'Well, where do I belong then?' 'Where are my people'? As Sam states, there is a recognition that it is all about the people, all about the FACES.

> I have moved around a lot since and feel a bit nomadic really – I have never felt like I fit in in England particularly

> *as it has not been very kind to me as a place. It was only recently I realised that belonging is about the people you love and who love you rather than a specific place.*
>
> (Sam)

Finding FACES

The importance of relationships is clear, but also what the FACES of those relationships mirror back has an impact on how a person sees them-selves. This can positively influence an individual's self-worth which is an important protective factor. Crystal elaborates on this idea further:

> *As I have grown older I have found belonging with peo-ple, sometimes it can be a moment, sometimes if I am lucky it can be longer. When I have found belonging, it's been felt, it's been like being wrapped in a blanket, it's a feeling of safety. When I have felt like I have belonged I have been able to identify myself in others, despite difference, and we have a shared acceptance of reality. Belonging is about that feeling of safety, of acceptance and that I am like you and you are like me and I will take care of you and your thoughts the way that you take care of mine. It's pure gold.*
>
> (Crystal)

Or as Maisie describes:

> *It's a feeling I feel like I belong 'cause I have people that accept me, people that they would judge me. People that don't shame me. I'm sure there's some of them around that do that still, but I have real people that don't.*
>
> (Maisie)

Finding belonging in intimate relationships is also raised by the participants, although it is difficult to decipher what enables the building of trust in intimate relationships where there has been early childhood neglect and abuse. Matthew and Shaun talk about belonging and trust:

> *And whilst belongings probably not the right word, I feel like myself and my partner belong together. So not we don't belong to each other, but we belong together, if that makes sense.*
>
> (Matthew)

> *We connect to each other ... I just I tell her everything and we do everything, like she was just my best friend. I don't bother with someone else.*
>
> (Shaun)

However, Crystal also emphasised that finding FACES was not a goal in itself: they did not have to try and be someone else in order to feel acceptance and therefore experience a sense of belonging.

> *I found my first sort of idea of belonging actually was that it was OK to be me, but I didn't need to try and be someone else.*
>
> (Crystal)

Nevertheless, for Donna, intimate relationships were not so straightforward:

> *My relationships were abusive so I've been on my own for a long time now because I didn't want my ... so I had two long term relationships, one where my older children came from and the other one where my youngest child came from and I just decided I can't do this 'cause I can't trust myself not to pick another person that is like*

that and I know, especially with my job, I know what the effect that had on my children.

(Donna)

Let's Take A Moment ...

- What does my body language say? Am I open? Do I come across as approachable? How do I know?
- When I smile is it genuine?
- Who smiles at me? Is it genuine?
- Have I grounded myself before I enter into relational practice?
- Am I prepared to keep showing up without expecting anything in return? Who fills my cup? Do I remember that nothing is personal?
- Relationships take time, consistency and emotional availability. Once achieved, the relationship is where the magic is.

Ultimately, we can see from the participant's experiences that simple acts of recognition such as remembering someone's name or nodding and smiling at a stranger can make a huge difference to someone's day. This also includes the intimate relationships we discuss. We can support the children and young people in our lives to gain a sense of community by joining inclusive activities in the local area and ensuring that the adults surrounding the child, where possible, are able to engage in warm interactions with the young person. After all, for many young people, particularly those who may have experienced trauma, the predictability and familiarity of FACES can be invaluable. The greater the number of members of a community that acknowledge children and young people, the greater the sense of belonging they will feel. Doing so in an authentic, non-tokenistic manner is also fundamental if connection is to follow.

Summary

Thinking about FACES that cultivate belonging is multi-layered and complex and can be hugely impactful. An understanding of FACES helps mirror to us that we belong and supports us in making an array of different connections, each serving its own purpose. FACES fuel our sense of community, acting as social landmarks even in situations where we may be new to the town. For some of us, frequent and consistent FACES help to reduce the negative impact that transient relationships can have, particularly on care-experienced young people.

Key Chapter Takeaways

- FACES goes far beyond the close relationships that most of us know are important but also reminds us of the power of familiar FACES within our community whom we may not know well.
- Regularity, not just depth of interactions, is important. Seeing familiar FACES often, even if we are only engaging in surface level/exchange-based interactions, are fundamental to our sense of belonging.
- Empathic reassurance and attunement from FACES we see often can cultivate greater psychological safety, contributing significantly to our sense of belonging.
- Finding belonging means we can be accepted for who we are and that we don't feel the need to change ourselves.

Reflection

Who are the FACES in your daily life that con-tribute to your sense of belonging? How do these interactions make you feel more connected to your community?

What does safety, attunement, connection and empathic reassurance look like from a FACE that a person doesn't know well?

How can you practise attunement and provide empathic reas-surance to others in your community?

How do these narratives enhance your understanding of the importance of FACES in cultivating a sense of belonging?

What does cultivating belonging look like from a person engaged in doing the deep work of trauma healing?

9

SPACES That Make a Difference

Introduction

SPACES refers to the inter-relational system. Let's take education as an example. Education, as a whole, is a SPACE. It provides an opportunity for belonging to be searched for and actively cultivated by those working or living in the SPACE. In education, we might argue that significant numbers of children and young people feel that they don't belong to that SPACE .... Education as a system makes going to school compulsory and is underpinned by a commitment to ensure that education is available to all. However, it does so against a background of reluctance to attend/non-attendance on the part of those who do not feel that they belong to the SPACE. I am not referring here to belonging to the PLACE, the school, as we will look at PLACES in the next chapter. Rather, I am thinking about those for whom formal education does not feel like a PLACE to belong to. A PLACE that may feel unsafe.

SPACES are socio-spatial which means they are both material and relational. They are shaped by cultural, economic and political forces which has an impact not only on how the SPACE is developed but also on how the meaning of the SPACE is interpreted by those who use it.

DOI: 10.4324/9781003426592-13

How can we cultivate belonging in a SPACE?

Safety – at the core

Pause – regular reflection

Awareness – of those who feel they don't belong

Connection – creating intentional relational webs

Embrace – the challenge

Being part of the system of care is, in this sense, a SPACE. In conceptualising space, Massey (2005) argues that space is inter-relational; it is a relational understanding of the world (p. 307). Furthering this idea of relationships with others, Low (2016) talks about space as something that can be embodied (p. 96), which arguably concerns the relationship we have with ourselves. Children in care might travel through numerous SPACES, as demonstrated in the findings of this research, and illuminated in earlier discussions about movement. Movement was a topic raised by every participant in the research.

Understanding SPACES as relational and embodied suggests that there is an urgent need to address the effects of movement and cultivate belonging. If it is the case that movement is unavoidable for children in care, then cultivating belonging is a major challenge, as belonging takes time to grow, and movement removes that opportunity. It is vital therefore that safety can be found in the FACES in those settings. We must also think about the construction of the SPACE. This is commented on by Alisha who considers the question of how to search for and then find belonging when there is such instability of FACES within the care system SPACE:

> *I think sometimes when you've gone through the care system and when you have corporate parents, you also don't really belong there because ultimately, foster carers can, it's a role for them. It's a job, so ultimately they have that choice to, you know, give you back if that makes sense.*
>
> (Alisha)

If we understand SPACE as being an inter-relational system, then it is not unreasonable to think of a country as a SPACE in the same way that we might think of a community.

> *I have never felt like I fit in in England particularly as it has not been very kind to me as a place.*
>
> (Sam)

Furthermore, the world itself can be seen as a SPACE which Donna did not feel she belonged to:

> *I didn't even believe that I belonged in the world. I felt that I shouldn't be here that somehow I was flawed and wasn't part of everything. I just didn't have a belonging. Does that make sense?*
>
> (Donna)

Another example of SPACE as a community is the connections made globally as accessed via social media, joining people together based on a single identity. There are so many groups online that offer a sense of community, of a shared SPACE, of connection. When I first started writing about adults who had experienced being in care as children for *The Brightness of Stars* (Cherry, 2013), it was not easy to find such people. Now there has been an explosion of groups, of networks, creating a sense of a 'care-experienced community' that provides a sense of belonging for many where that simply may not have been possible before. As Crystal explains:

> I think for me I've I found my biggest sense of belonging and inclusion as an adult, and that has been through the care experience community because there are so many themes that run through in my life that resonate, that actually they don't – that most people don't get or they think they get and they really don't. So it's almost like they're normative.
>
> (Crystal)

In practice, in addition to ensuring the presence of consistent FACES to populate the SPACES children and young people frequent, there are some really invaluable activities we can also invite them to participate in. Some children find comfort in populating their SPACES with photographs or artwork which can serve as a visual reminder of belonging. If we are able to apply the principles of trauma-informed practice to the design of the SPACE, it might be worth considering having safe zones where children and young people who feel overwhelmed can go without question. This can help children keep a sense of control within the SPACE.

Movement

Having concluded that the level of movement of children in care appears unavoidable, it is essential to cultivate belonging in the SPACES they inhabit. Understanding SPACES as relational and embodied suggests an urgency in mitigating the effects of movement and cultivating belonging. Ideally, movement and cultivating belonging should go hand in hand but searching for belonging is also tied up with feeling deserving of belonging. This means that those who are working with children and young people not only develop intentional mechanisms to cultivate belonging but also that some work is done to build self esteem to ensure that belonging is something children and young people deserve. Creating safety is not the same as someone feeling safe, and belonging is no different. Cultivating belonging does not automatically mean that a person feels they belong. Participating in familiar pursuits can provide, for example, support for children after a move to re-establish getting involved with some of their hobbies or interests in their new area. The familiarity here can provide comfort for many. For some children, becoming part of peer support groups where they can share their experiences with other children can be beneficial. To be more specific, we must be led by the child ... always. Sometimes children do not know what they need. In these situations, we can gently guide and make suggestions about what is often useful.

However, establishing and understanding that movement is unavoidable for children in care presents a real challenge around how belonging can be cultivated. Belonging takes time to grow, yet movement removes that opportunity. It is vital therefore that safety can be detected in the FACES in those settings and that the construction of the setting invites belonging. One example, is in discussions of 'school', generically:

> I think you as a young person, you're always trying to belong and you're trying to find your identity. And I think the school is pivotal for that and it's reinforcement, it's people believing in you.
>
> (Jenny)

Or, when one is not encouraged to belong:

> The same goes for school. All you want at that age is to fit in, to be unremarkable, to blend in. Yet, you're marked out as different by being in care. That's just the teachers! They have a pretty dim view of you before you've even opened your mouth.
>
> (Matthew)

Thinking about SPACES broadens the sense of opportunities offered by an environment, for example, by emphasising the scope for movement and the potential for active adaptation to the needs and agency of those entering and experiencing it. The experience of a SPACE can be impacted by the entrance into that SPACE.

Finding Belonging

It is now widely understood and accepted that we arrive in the world hard wired to connect to our caregivers and the community that awaits us. When we cannot access that connection, the consequences, for those who survive it, cast a long shadow that extends far beyond a miserable childhood. Research in the last century looking at infant mortality and orphanages found that a lack of love can be the cause of infant death (Spitz, 1949). However, efforts dedicated to understanding the need for love in order for a baby to have the best chance of survival and to flourish continues (Tronick, 2007; Szalavitz and Perry, 2010; Gerhardt, 2015). It would seem society needs to be constantly reminded of the importance of the need for love. The participants from my research have gifted us with the knowledge that 'belonging connectors' such as touch, acceptance and a sense of safety are critical. This makes distinguishing between love, belonging, touch, connection, acceptance and psychological and physical safety challenging.

Let's Take A Moment …

Do I understand and recognise that SPACES that purport to be inclusive can be very excluding? In what ways do I work to avoid that being the case?

Am I looking for strengths and talents within the child that the SPACE might not validate? As Einstein is famously reported

---

to have said, 'Everybody is a genius. But if you judge a fish by its ability to climb a tree, it will live its whole life believing that it is stupid.'

What can I change?

When I get overwhelmed, who supports me? How do I support myself?

Summary

Searching for belonging is a human motivation that can be fractured through the experiences of being in care and being excluded from school. The development of belonging in children is inextricably linked to them forming identities with internal narratives about deserving belonging and self-worth . Searching for belonging in the FACES, SPACES and PLACES that are available for those in care as children is complicated because movement is an inevitable aspect of that situation. This means that it is vital to cultivate belonging as an active and deliberate centralised theme of professional practice which seeks to ensure that, at the very least, the experience of belonging is experienced by the children and young people affected.

Key Chapter Takeaways

- SPACES are shaped by layered processes and each will contribute to an individual's felt sense of belonging in different ways.
- As adults, we can support the deliberate but careful creation of relational webs to support connection.
- We must be aware that movement can impede belonging but there is a lot that can be done to mitigate these effects.

- Applying trauma-informed principles to the design of our SPACE contributes to psychological safety, and subsequently a sense of belonging, but this isn't a simple process that can be rushed.

Reflection

How can the design of physical and relational SPACES impact an individual's sense of belonging, and what processes should be considered to enhance this sense of belonging?

In what ways can the principles of trauma-informed design be applied to create SPACES that foster psychological safety, and what challenges might arise in trying to implement these principles thoughtfully?

How can adults support the careful creation of relational webs to foster a sense of connection, and what strategies can be used to mitigate the negative effects of movement or change within these SPACES?

References and Bibliography

Cherry, L. (2013). *The Brightness of Stars: Stories of Adults Who Came through the British Care System*. Banbury: Wilson King Publishing.

Gerhardt, S. (2015). *Why Love Matters: How Affection Shapes a Baby's Brain* (2nd ed.). New York: Taylor & Francis.

Low, S. M. (2016). *Spatializing Culture: The Ethnography of Space and Place*. New York: Routledge.

Massey, D. B. (2005). *For Space*. London: SAGE.

Smith, M., Cameron, C., & Reimer, D. (2017). From attachment to recognition for children in care. *British Journal of Social Work,* 47: 1606–1623.

Spitz, R. A. (1949). The role of ecological factors in emotional development in infancy. *Child Development,* 20(3): 145–155.

Szalavitz, M., & Perry, B. D. (2010). *Born for Love: Why Empathy is Essential – and Endangered.* New York: Harper Collins.

Tronick, E. (2007). *The Neurobehavioral and Social-emotional Development of Infants and Children* (1st ed.). New York: W.W. Norton & Co.

10
PLACES That Make a Difference

Introduction

FACE refers to relationships, SPACE refers to the system such as education or children's services and the idea of PLACE captures the particular context as manifestations of SPACE such as a school, a community home or a foster home. As Massey remarks about PLACE, 'there is, then, an issue of whose identity we are referring to when we talk of a place called home and of the supports it may provide of stability, oneness and security' (Massey, 2018, p. 169). For Alisha, belonging itself *is* the PLACE!

DOI: 10.4324/9781003426592-14

*I think belonging is a safe place and that's my under-
standing of belonging is that it's nurturing, it's safe, it's
warm, it's a place where we all want to have a place
where we feel we belong. But for myself, I feel that's
something that I constantly strive for.*

(Alisha)

In cultivating belonging in PLACE, the model asks us to consider how
we intentionally create relational networks through peer support. Is
it a listening PLACE? How accessible is it? Do we resonate with one
another? Do you understand me? PLACE also needs to observe cultural humility through understanding that we cannot know what we
have not lived. Finally, is the PLACE reflective and safe?

How might we cultivate belonging in a PLACE?

Peer support – intentional

Listening – am I heard?

Accessibility – can I see me in you?

Cultural humility

Environment – safe, reflective

Examples of places can be very explicit, as they are for James:

*I had 10 very good years in a small community home,
a small family group home. Then aged 10, the woman
who ran the home was made redundant or asked to
leave and my whole world fell apart and my behaviour
really changed.*

(James)

The impact of a lack of PLACE can be devastating, highlighting the need to think about how FACES and PLACES work together to cultivate belonging. Some participants recognised the importance of this without having experienced it:

> I guess for some people maybe that have more of a permanent place in school and in a care home rather than being moved a lot, having that one person in each place that you feel safe with is probably going to help as well, but I think you need to start with one person.
>
> (Maisie)

However, a potentially beneficial SPACE could be negated by a particular PLACE. Jenny found the SPACE of education difficult because of the particular school they attended:

> So I found myself going to a school that was quite affluent where there was, you know, people not from their typical broken homes, but both parents drove them to school. They have the latest gear. You know, they would sit at a table and eat. And so I already … and then I was kind of the only brown child in there.
>
> (Jenny)

As Sam shows, different types of PLACE can be more or less beneficial:

> As I never fitted into mainstream school I was sent to small centres and when I was forced to leave those, I took overdoses and tried to go back to them. I think in those places it was more like a family so I felt like I belonged more. In the big schools I was nobody.
>
> (Sam)

This is not a rejection of education, but of a particular school, valuing instead the other 'small centres'. Participants also point to how the image of a PLACE can affect their experience of belonging:

> I remember well the feelings of not belonging that came from being called names and never feeling anyone defended me or understood why I was so angry. I was excluded from primary school aged 9 and sent to a boarding school for mal-adjusted kids. I cried and begged my social worker not to take me there because I knew it was where all the bad kids from my town went.
>
> (James)

James highlights the powerlessness experienced when everyone in your life is paid to be there, which means they can disappear either temporarily, for example if they go on holiday, or permanently, as they can be fired or simply leave for a variety of other reasons. PLACES can be schools, care homes or foster families and it is PLACES which further reinforce the idea that belonging is possible if you can find the right FACES and SPACES within them. PLACES further reinforce the idea that belonging is possible if you can find the right FACES and SPACES within them. Finally, for Jenny, belonging is a longer-term commitment which school can determine:

> I think you, as a young person, you're always trying to belong and you're trying to find your identity. And I think the school is pivotal for that and it's reinforcement, it's people believing in you.
>
> (Jenny)

Let's Take A Moment …

Do I understand the role of the environment in creating a PLACE that cultivates belonging? What is on the wall? Are the seats comfortable?

How do I incorporate 'I do not know what I have not lived' in the environment?

Have I considered co-creating the PLACE we share?

Do I understand that I do not have all the answers but I have the power to make a difference when we all work together?

Summary

This chapter has considered the concept of FACE, SPACE and PLACE in cultivating belonging for children and young people. FACE helps us to remember the key aspects of building relationships, SPACE refers to systems like education or children's services and PLACE involves specific contexts such as schools or foster homes. PLACES can contribute to nurturing belonging because children and young people are more likely to feel understood and valued. For this reason we must be intentional with our practice of creating networks, thinking about how we can be culturally humble and prioritise safety above all else.

Key Chapter Takeaways

- Getting our environments right is vital to ensure that all young people feel seen and valued.
- Working intentionally means we can weave belonging through all we do.
- We cannot know what we have not lived, instead we can seek to understand through being present in the moment with a child or young person.

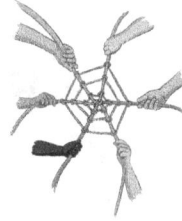

Reflection

What role could play take in creating a PLACE that promotes belonging for everyone in it?

Think of a time when you were in a PLACE where you felt like you belonged. How do you think it achieved that for you and is there anything from the experience that could translate into your own practice?

Bibliography

Massey, D. B. (2018). *The Doreen Massey Reader* (B. Christophers. R. Lave, J. Peck, & M. Werner, Eds.). Newcastle upon Tyne: Agenda Publishing.

11

Beyond Practice

Introduction

This chapter is dedicated to my belief that belonging, relationships and connection should be central to policy because they shape how we practise and how we support children and young people. The language used in policies – whether in education, safeguarding or care –can create a more compassionate and effective system. By shifting from terms that stigmatise to those that foster acceptance, we can transform how young people see themselves and how we work with them, especially those without strong support networks. Drawing on examples from countries such as Australia and Canada, I advocate for a focus on belonging and interdependence, which could lead to more supportive transitions and better outcomes for those in care.

Doing Better in Policy

I have sought to argue that belonging, relationships and relationality need to be at the core of policy so they can, in turn, shape practice. Policy can drive practice so it is important that the language used in policy creates the world we wish to see. Words such as belonging, relationships, connection and compassion in policies regarding education, safeguarding, school exclusion and children in care would create better services. In Chapter 6, I argued that language in legislation

DOI: 10.4324/9781003426592-15

filters into policy and then into how practitioners speak about and to children and young people. This language is internalised and shapes internal narratives. Imagine what could change if we changed the language in policy! It would create different types of practice, and different ways of responding and working with children and young people who do not have lots of supportive loving relationships around them.

Centralising belonging in how we think about young people leaving care would completely change the narrative of 'independence' to an understanding of 'interdependence', with development of a relational web at the core. A supportive transition out of care would take more of a life course perspective and embed relationality/relationships in that process. Policies lack the term 'belonging' in this country but it can be found elsewhere, notably in some Australian and Canadian policies which set out the importance of belonging, and in a manner which accounts for the diversity of world views, of cultural and socio-economic context and of personal experiences. Being colonised as opposed to being the coloniser needs to be considered when we write policies as the legacies of colonialism (such as in Australia and Canada) bring to the fore a repeated pattern of stolen generations. Indigenous children and families are taught by elders and scholars about belonging – belonging to country, belonging to land, belonging to each other. That said, there has been a recent shift in England. Children's services now include a 'staying put' agenda, which relates to being able to stay put with one's foster carers. The recent independent care review talked about love, and, even if many are unconvinced that this will not result in real change, it is nonetheless being expressed in the policy language.

I have argued that belonging can be seen as an antidote to trauma and that language matters. Currently, phrases like: 'hard to reach', 'looked after child', 'child in need', 'excluded' and 'hard to engage' pepper practitioner speak and the written word. But there is an opportunity to form a different narrative, a different way of understanding experiences, a different way of thinking about what it means to be someone who uses services. Not the waifs and strays of the 19th century, but children who have a right to belong in their community, in some sort of family where they are protected.

If 'belonging' becomes part of policy language, and is one part of the lexicon by which people describe themselves, this could benefit them in terms of their self-understanding, thereby reducing self stigma and social stigma. The language set out above would suggest that the 'problem is me', and so language is needed that enables young people to understand they are accepted just as they are. Children and young people do not have to grow up thinking they are the problem. Collectively we have an opportunity to develop an entirely different way that people can think about themselves and their experience within a system that does not problematise the individual.

We need a balance of curiosity and responsibility in our use of language when describing the myriad experiences that someone has had. Currently, educational systems are an inequitable PLACE for trauma-affected students because the likelihood of being able to meet 'mainstream milestones' when you are also living with, dealing with, responding to and healing from trauma is not the priority. As such, methods to eliminate the barriers must be sought out so that those in care are able to access education at their own pace across their life course.

In summary, we need to consider better relationships, including post service and also the adoption of a life course perspective in policy, as well as professional development and working conditions. These policies should look at the workforce, the care providers and the children. The kind of normative framings that are not deficit narratives must be changed. These narratives need to be constructed through policies that seep into practice, to be co-constructed with the beneficiaries of the services rather than being above and external to them and to re-balance the burden of responsibility between the individual, the service and society more broadly. Given that policy drives practice, we turn there next.

Doing Better in Practice

Chapters 8, 9 and 10 have offered a conceptual model to support practice 'in practice' highlighting the importance of FACES, PLACES and SPACES. Put differently, an ecological system that focuses on relational webs of support that go beyond the service is essential to cultivating belonging. When we talk about relationships, we are referring to prior relationships and recognising ongoing relationships. However, we are also talking about post-service relationships, which are particularly important.

The objective is to ensure that part of our work is developing relational webs for those children and young people in a community, whether that is looking at extracurricular activities, involvement in the community or ensuring children are not housed or schooled outside of their community. Clearly this is a political issue, locally and nationally, not simply a practice issue. However, driving change can come from all angles and legislation dances with public attitudes.

In order to do this work of relational web building, we must take care of the people doing the work and this needs to be done properly, they, in turn, can cultivate what is required to achieve a sense of belonging for children and young people. Professional and care relationships matter and we cannot starve systems, fail to look after those who work in them and then get upset that systems have poor retention, high staff turnover, burnout, sickness and the children and young people within those SPACES have no relationships to access post-service.

In summary, recognising the importance of relationships and of different types of relationships with other people is vital. Mechanisms need to be put in place that enable relationships to be sustained over time and across different settings. There needs to be flexibility, while ensuring safety that enables professional judgement to override narrowly defined structures which can sometimes mean that relational working is impossible. Finally, we need to ensure good working conditions and professional development for those charged with the care and education of children in care, building care into the ethos of the work.

Doing Better in Research

Research needs to develop so that people can be thought about as having intersectional and interrelated experiences, and not just a person with one identity that is experienced in isolation from all the other identities that we carry. The understanding that children become adults, and adults were once children, needs to be incorporated into policy, practice *and* research. We need to acknowledge the diversity of the population we are discussing. Taking a life course perspective enables self-definitions for belonging to be formed as adults make sense of their journeys and begin families themselves. Belonging gives parity to going both downstream (prevention) and upstream (where the harm has already happened). There are broader implications for research on belonging which speaks to our fundamental human need to connect with one another. If we get it right for the people where it really matters, then we get it right for everybody. This research implies a need for a collective understanding of taking responsibility for cultivating belonging. We can further consider the structural and spatial implications of how a community is designed to enable a sense of belonging, and geography as a discipline may offer insights into this.

Summary

In this chapter, the emphasis is on belonging and relationships within the sphere of policy in recognition of the fact that policy directly informs our practice. A great starting point is to review the language used by policy makers, ensuring we take steps towards making this much more compassionate. This is integral to transforming how we work with children and young people in our practice. Here, I argue for a narrative shift from independence to interdependence, advocating for much more support around transitions. Why? Because weaving belonging through policy will improve the outcomes for marginalised groups as we will all be held collectively accountable. Finally, I also call for research that acknowledges the intersectional experiences of individuals within not only policy and practice, but also community design to cultivate a holistic approach to creating opportunities to promote belonging.

Key Chapter Takeaways

- Relational practice must be weaved through all relevant policy documents and this shift must subsequently be integrated into all of our practice with children and young people.
- Shifting our language use within all documentation shifts the dynamic and will contribute towards destigmatisation.
- Championing the professional development of caregivers and ensuring they receive the support they require will, in turn, reduce burnout rates whilst increasing retention.
- A collective effort is needed on a policy, practice and community-based model if children and young people are to feel the benefit of our 'weaving' of belonging.

Reflection

What insights can you draw upon from this chapter?

What changes can be made to your community structure to promote belonging more profoundly?

What partnerships might support you to feel an increased sense of belonging within the SPACES and PLACES that you use? (This might be personal or professional.)

How can you ensure that you are informed by research within your practice?

12
Closing Words

Adults who support children and young people who have experienced trauma tend to offer solutions which may be of more use to adults. For example, talking therapies which require a cognitive and articulate use of language to express internal distress using a vocabulary that many adults do not possess. Therefore, the demand for school counsellors can be heard far and wide as these professionals offer therapeutic support in age-appropriate ways. However, it is important that we don't fix our sights on school counsellors alone. There are also many other 'interventions' that can service children's wellbeing which could include: play, music, drama, sport and any other activity that releases the build-up of toxic stress as this provides an outlet and opportunity for mastery of these activities and has an inbuilt relationship growth mechanism. In other words, what those activities also provide is an opportunity to extend the relational network which builds relational wealth. Basically, these activities hold the key to positive and healthy experiences of belonging.

Inviting you to think about belonging through reading this book, has left me trying to make sense of my own mortality, which invariably called me to question my own sense of belonging yet again. Belonging has been a lifelong query which has formed the soundtrack to my life, annoyingly posing questions that I wish I had understood at the time they were posed.

As I entered into the last couple of chapters of my doctorate at the end of 2023, having already signed the contract to write this book, I

DOI: 10.4324/9781003426592-16

was diagnosed with an incurable, yet treatable cancer known as mul-tiple myeloma. It is a blood cancer, lying dormant in the bone mar-row until it can no longer keep itself to itself. It causes bone pain and lesions in several bones around the body, kidney damage and fatigue. The causes are unknown and as someone who has spent a lifetime taking care of myself through not having a drink since 1990, not smok-ing since 2005, eating non-processed foods for decades and being a regular gym goer who loved to walk everywhere, it was a shock. There was one thing I hadn't tended to however. Well, rather than hadn't tended to, I should say that I am in the process of seeing to it even though I had understood it wasn't always much of an option. Stress. Invariably the kind of stress that happens when you live with relational poverty. Raising a family, predominantly alone and without any family support, is not how raising a family is meant to be. We are meant to raise families as villages but we don't. We are meant to notice when a woman is crying in a coffee shop trying to manage the logistics of a baby and a toddler who are both crying too and have managed to knock the drinks off the table. But we don't. In fact, invariably we judge. If we take the coffee shop incident, and yes that was me crying in the coffee shop, and we broaden that out to think about how we culturally respond to poor housing, poverty and mental illness, for example, then weaving relational webs, considering com-munity responses to distress and the cultivation of belonging becomes a public health issue. There is no point housing someone without also ensuring that they have someone to invite around for a cup of tea and the skills to help them invite that person around again.

I am very deeply tangled up in this writing as we all are in our work and our life. We all have a motivational need to belong and we will all have experienced the sensation of not belonging, whether that was in a fundamental aspect of our lives such as what has been described in this book or something somewhat smaller. We share that sense of loss on some level.

In writing a book about belonging which is essentially aimed at those working in education, children's services and voluntary and community sector settings, I hope that together, we can support all children and young people to make the meaning that matters most to them with regard to the FACES, SPACES and PLACES that make up the canvas of their life.

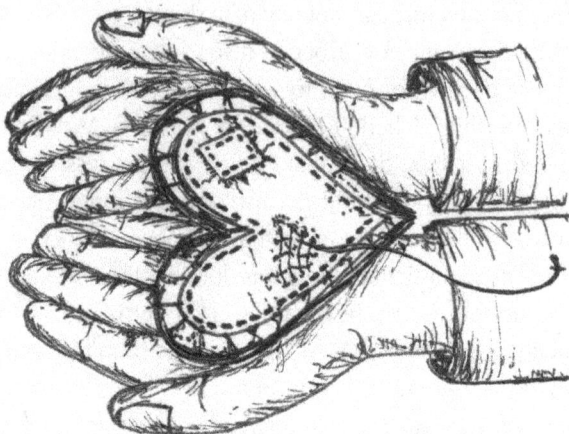

Prologue

Everywhere
Belonging, met in the place
visited briefly, a person who
remembered us, the friendly
face, a welcome home
even when they knew

we had never visited this
place before, a show of kindness
welcoming words, an open
heart, inviting spaces to be still,
not expected to repeat

life stories in all our phases
acceptance met, upon
return, our hearts belonged
loved unconditionally, the
welcome, remains lifelong.

(Chrissy Kelly,
Care-experienced poet)

Index

For Product Safety Concerns and Information please contact our EU
representative GPSR@taylorandfrancis.com
Taylor & Francis Verlag GmbH, Kaufingerstraße 24, 80331 München, Germany

www.ingramcontent.com/pod-product-compliance
Lightning Source LLC
Chambersburg PA
CBHW061733270326
41928CB00011B/2221